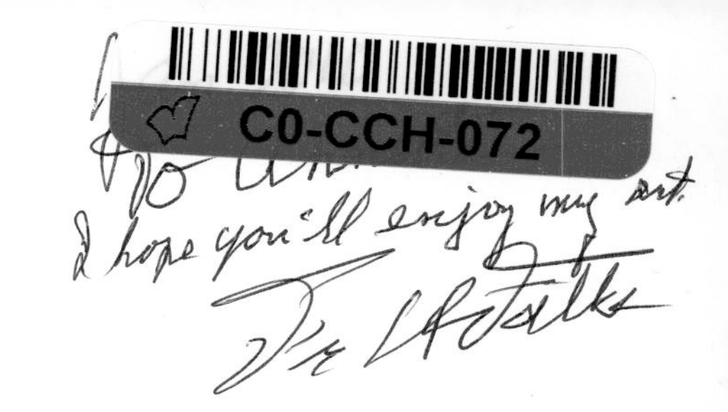

P.S. There's More

Latest Gleanings of my Sculptures and Paintings

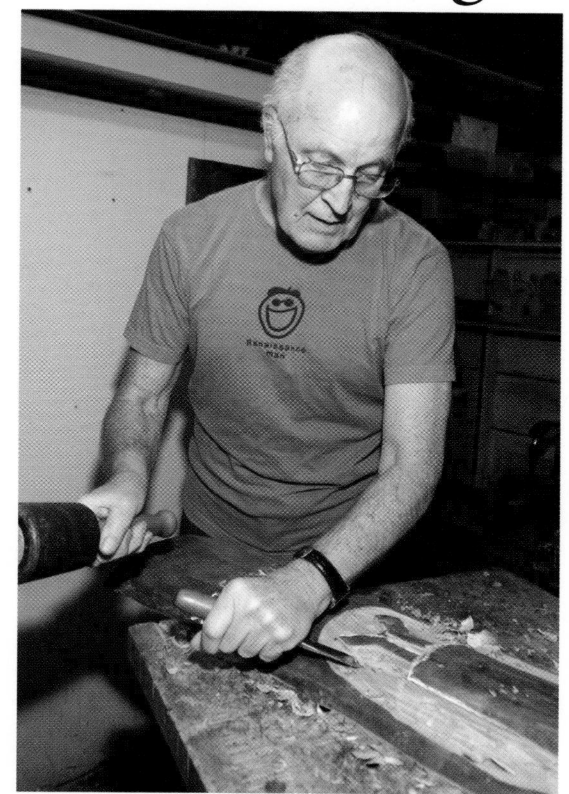

Fr. Herman Falke

Commoners' Publishing
Ottawa Canada
2009

Published by
Commoners Publishing
631 Tubman Cr.
Ottawa, Canada K1V 8L6
(613) 523-2444
fax: (613) 260-0401
editor@commonerspublishing.com
www.commonerspublishing.com

ERRATA:

pg	*should read*
6	yourself
7	accidentally
7	unnumbered art (3A)
15	delete single quote
19	for
20	this
21	jingle
34&35	prodigal
49	sorrowful
65	sculpture
91	sticks
127	particularly
137	to the

Acknowledgements:

Photography of selected art by Jean Paul Picard

Library and Archives Canada Cataloguing in Publication

Falke, Herman
P.S. there's more : latest gleanings of my sculpture and paintings / Herman Falke.

Includes index.
ISBN 978-0-88970-135-9

1. Falke, Herman. I. Title.

NB249.F35A4 2009 730.92 C2009-907167-3

Printed and bound in Canada

#1 ❋ (front cover) Ruth is cleaning wheat off Boaz's field, and in the process catches a husband: Boaz

❋ Red ornament indicates additional information is available on Annotations, page 157

www.hermanfalke.com
192 Daly Avenue,
Ottawa, K1N 6E9
cell: 613-371-7793

Contents

#2 In the Light of Understanding, Specters Evaporate

Preface

It is my privilege and honour to extend to Father Falke our most sincere thanks for his 18 years of pastoral service to St. Brigid's. Also we wish to express our delight and gratitude that he will remain with us, continuing his work, for at least another year or so at which time we hope St. Brigid's will become part of a shared ministry of five Sacred Heart Fathers in the Ottawa Archdiocese. Our spiritual and temporal lives have been vastly enriched by Father's devoted care and this latest record of his artistic genius will be a treasured keepsake for each parish .

God bless you, Father Falke and we wish you health and happiness for years to come.

Peter Kelly

We Journey in Hope

As St. John the Evangelist and St. Catherine of Siena join together as a united parish, we are mindful of our shared heritage as mission churches in the 1850's, and that our roots are deep in Enniskerry and Metcalfe. Our Catholic community in rural south Ottawa is built upon the strong foundation of our pioneer families and our early pastors, their perseverance and their hope for the future. The fact that we continue to flourish is a testament to the strength of our faith; like our forefathers, we adapt and continue to come together to worship, to welcome and to minister to one another.

Together, St. Catherine and St. John can look to our future with confidence, knowing where we have come from, who we are, and all that we can be. Inspired by Psalm 92, we know that:

> "The just will grow as tall as palms,
> Like cedars they shall stand,
> And planted firmly on their God,
> They shall not break or bow."
> We journey together in hope!

Mark O'Neill

January 2010 - a historical footnote

Suddenly, when this book was already being printed, the Ottawa Diocese called off the joining of St. John's and St. Catherine's.

For us small rural parishes, there remains a painful awareness that the continuing shortage of priests may necessitate some form of amalgamation in the future.

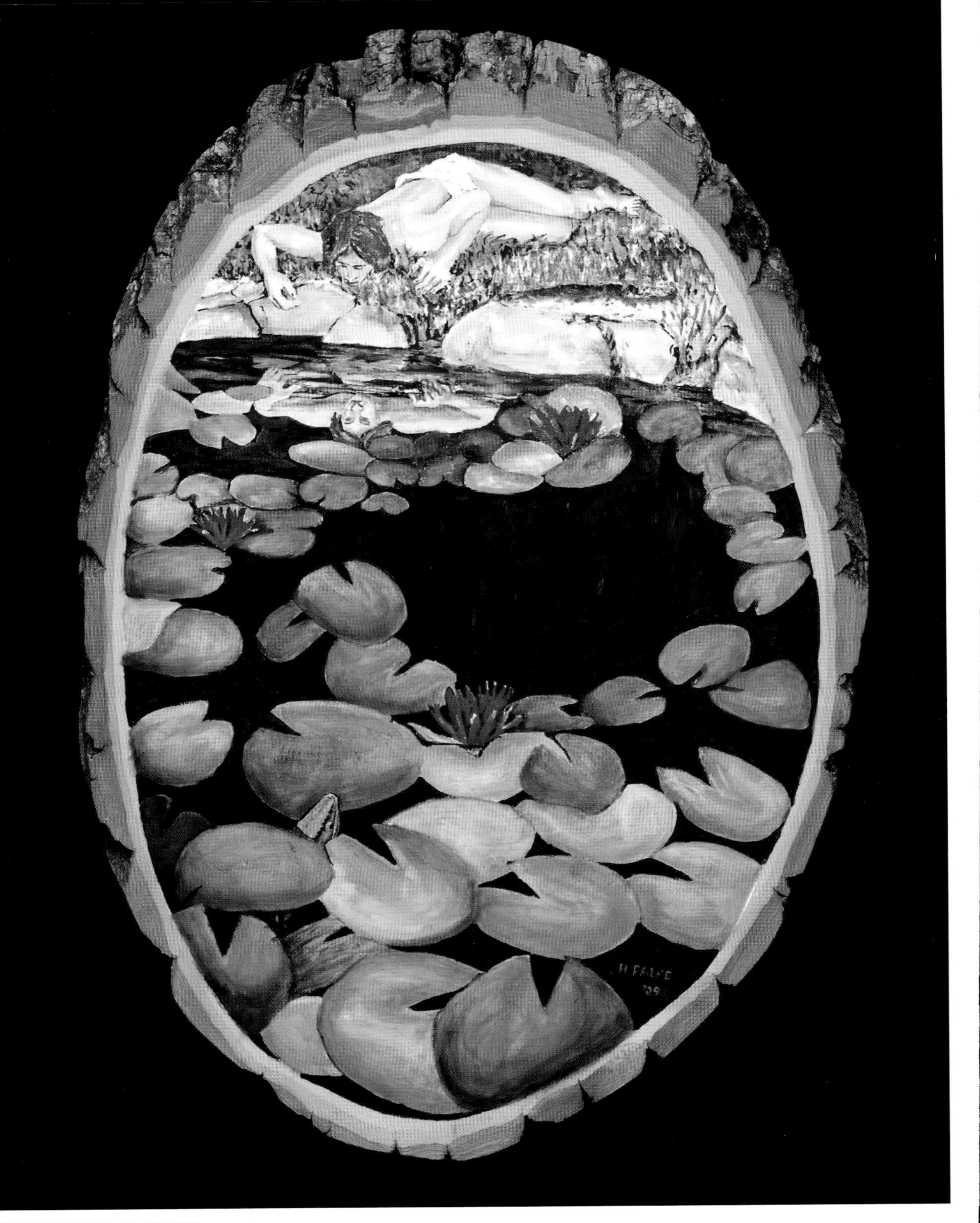

#3 Falling in love with oneself can be foolish and dangerous, as Narcissus of Greek mythology experienced to the point of getting drowned. You do not have to hide yoruself and your gifts, but let others be the judges.

Introduction

My desire and subsequent pleasure in creating a continuous supply of sculptures and paintings has been carried by four motivations, arranged in their order of importance:

1. To bring religion and specifically sacred scriptures to an understandable level by way of visible and tangible images,
2. To testify to the beauty of our world, including the human development of it,
3. To find meaning in happenings in our time,
4. To let others share in my personal appreciation of beauty, even sensual beauty.

During this year of 2010 I am turning 82. I feel a bit like a squirrel at the onset of fall: get those nuts stored away before they are covered up by leaves and snow.

Up to the present day I have experienced a steady stream of creativity, lately especially in painting, which produces much faster results than sculpture. This book will show some 60 paintings, half of them those popular Canadian landscapes on oval willow slices, like the one above.

Moreover, in old age you start to drastically reduce accumulated treasures: portfolios of sketches, old photographs, and boxes of slides that nobody ever looks at. Out of maybe 3000 slides, I've kept one box of 80, half of which I had my photographer turn into photos. To use a mixed metaphor, these final 40 photos broke the camel's back of my resistance to publishing another book about my art in spite of the fact that my previous book of 2008 was titled "Swan Songs". Indeed, there's more.

An added motivation for this book is the sense of nostalgia and gratitude that arises from having been allowed 18 years of pastoral ministry in Osgoode Township that has come to an end for St. John's in December 2009, while at St. Brigid's it is still somewhere in the foreseeable future.

Herman Falke, Ottawa, December 2009

Gleanings: when harvesting grain, some ears are accidentally overlooked. Gathering them up is gleaning.

The Old Testament, or Hebrew Scriptures

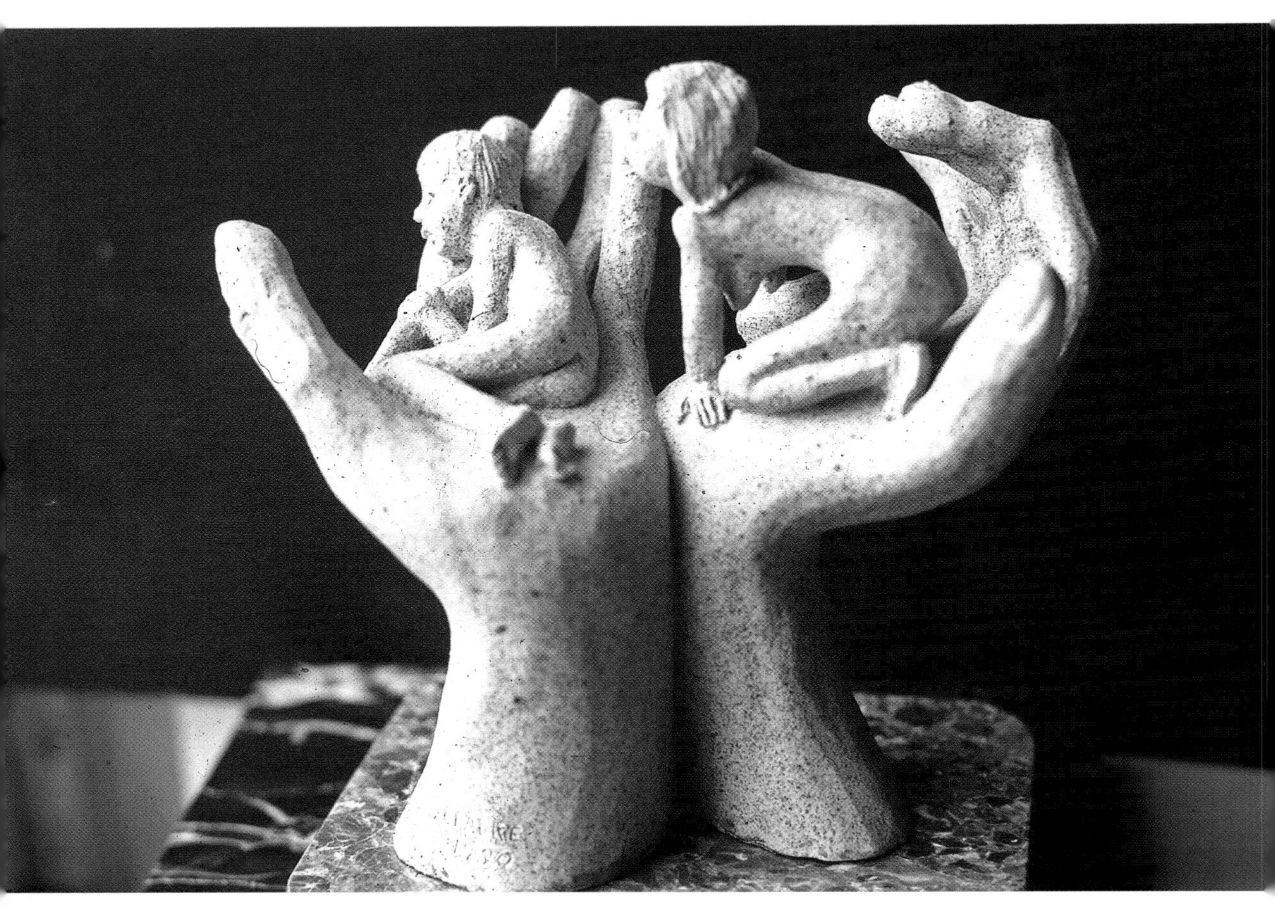

#4 Adam and Eve at the dawn of their creation, still in God's hands.

Red ornament indicates additional information is available on Annotations, page 157

 #5

#6-9 Story of Adam and Eve in four sculptures

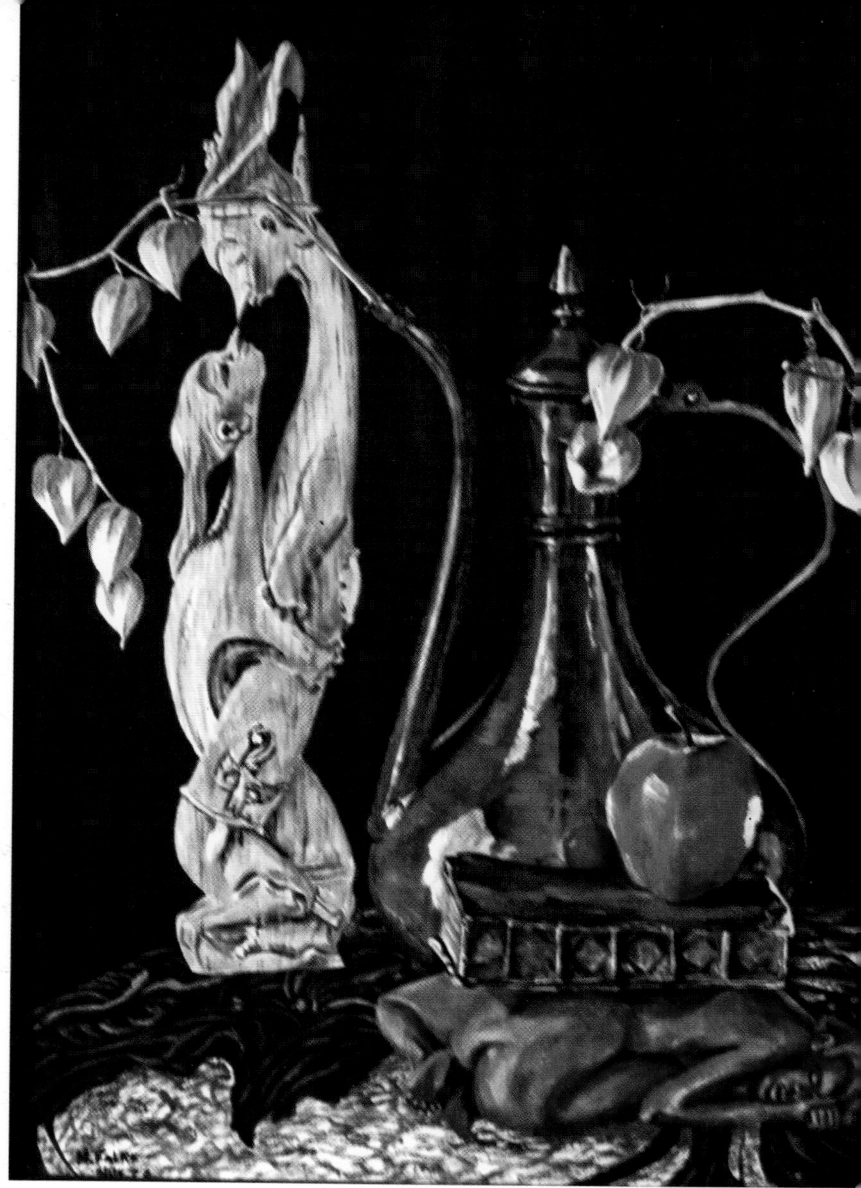

#10 Still life Eve with apple

By way of exception I set up for myself a still life with a vaguely spiritual theme. It was probably the tall Indonesian woodcarving in the back that triggered this, because it seemed to suggest male dominance. An antique bible that is somehow weighing down on a contrite Eve, and an apple with one bite taken out, supplement a somewhat wishy-washy religious idea.

My third version of "Adam and Eve after their fall" is in stoneware. It has in common with the other two versions which were featured in my previous two books, that gesture of holding each other's hand. In spite of their failures and embarrassment, they intend to carry on with each other's support.

The four black-and-white photos represent the four sides of a pedestal for a sculpture of Adam and Eve. They picture four highlights of their lives, namely the creation of Eve from Adam's rib, their temptation under the fruit tree, their hiding from God, and their later existence as tillers of the soil.

Lot and family escaping from Sodom

#11

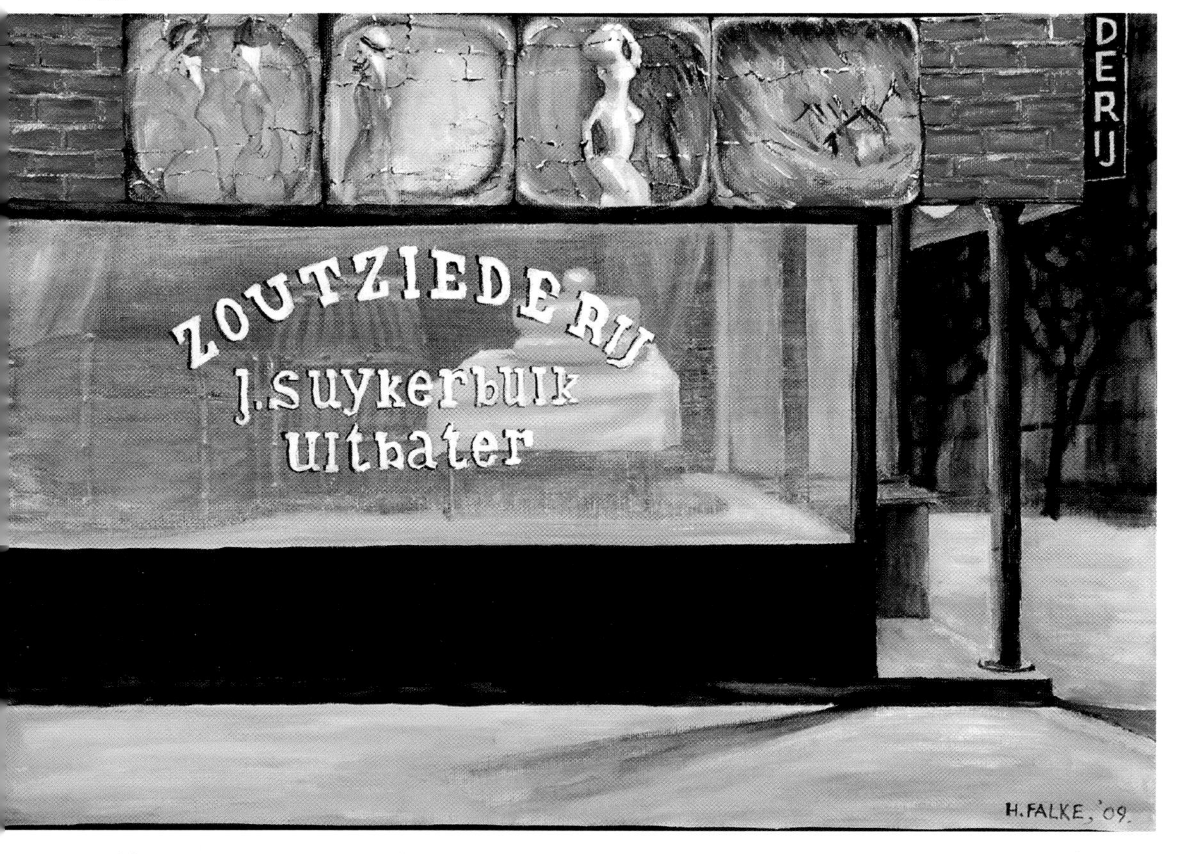

Half a century ago, many businesses and prominent homes in Europe used to install near their front entrance a religious stone or ceramic sculpture. Most often it was a Madonna and child, and sometimes a popular saint like St. Francis. A carpenter would have a St . Joseph sculpture. I have produced all the above for family and friends.

Here is an imaginative businessman in Amsterdam who happened to refine salt for industries that produce butter, cheese, or fish. He used the biblical story of Lot and his family from Genesis, chapters 18 & 19. God is destroying by fire the sinful towns of Sodom and Gomorrah in the Dead Sea area. The only righteous citizens who are allowed to escape are Lot, his wife, and their two daughters, under the one condition that they flee without looking back. Lot's wife cannot resist a look back, and is turned into a pillar of salt.

Ancient stories like this one probably arose from a desire to explain the geological origin of the Dead Sea and its freaky salt formations.

#12

Jacob's ladder

It may astound us to read in the Bible how God often favours weak people. The Patriarch Jacob is a good example.

As a young man he tricked his brother Esau out of his first-birth rights for a bowl of soup. He also tricked his blind father Isaac. Then he was forced to flee for his life. During one night of his escape, Jacob had a dream: he saw a ladder between earth and heaven, with angels ascending and descending along the ladder. The ascending angels carried to the throne of God Jacob's guilt and remorse over all that had gone wrong in his life, and his fear and insecurity over his unknown future.

The descending angels carried God's mercy and encouragement. (Genesis 28:10-22)

#13

Story of Joseph in Egypt

A quarter of Genesis is taken up by the story of Joseph in Egypt.

It is a high point in world literature as it deals with the theme of humiliation versus exaltation.

The sculpture is constructed from the bottom up. The young Joseph is naive enough to tell his brothers a dream in which his sheaf of wheat was standing upright while those of his ten brothers bowed deeply to him.

His brothers started to hate him and managed to sell him into Egyptian slavery. There his correct and astute interpretation of Pharaoh's dream of seven fat cows followed by seven lean ones gained him the high position of viceroy, in charge of storing surplus grain for the seven lean years to come.

The upper three scenes deal with the painful testing of the ten brothers, and final reconciliation.

Christians have often interpreted Joseph as foreshadowing Jesus, the rejected redeemer.

Balaam and his speaking donkey

#14

Here is one of the strangest stories of the old Bible, actually a legend with elements of a fable. It takes up three chapters of the Book of Numbers.

The king of Moab felt threatened when the twelve tribes of Israelites passed through his territory on their way from Egypt to the Promised land. So he looked for the prophet Balaam who had the reputation of having effective curses. 'The king promised Balaam rich rewards if he would curse the Israelites.

So Balaam set out on his donkey, although God had warned him, "do not put a curse on the Israelites because they have my blessing…" (Nu: 22:12). On the road, an angel blocks his way with a sword, but only the donkey sees him, goes through his front legs and crushes Balaam's leg against a stone wall. Balaam loses his temper and beats the donkey mercilessly with his stick. "I have served you all my life," says the donkey, "why do you beat me?"

That opened Balaam's eyes, and then he sees the angel. Instead of cursing the Israelites, he blesses them, as God had made him understand by way of the talking donkey.

#15 The Song of Songs

"THE SONG OF SONGS" is a series of love poems that describes the wonder of the love between two young people who sing about each other's beauty and goodness. They experience how they are drawn to each other like magnets.

> You are graceful as a palm tree,
> and your breasts are clusters of dates.
> I will climb the palm tree and pick its fruit.

Bible scholars who may have been inclined to prudish reluctance in accepting the "Song of Songs" as one of the Sacred Books of Scripture, may interpret these songs as a picture of the relationship between Christ and the Church.

Others see in them a reflection of chapter two of Genesis that describes the creation of man and woman. When God created Eve from Adam's rib, Adam cried out in rapture "at last, here is one of my own kind – bone taken from my bone, and flesh from my flesh." Gen 2:23.

Adam's thanksgiving is elaborated in "The Song of Songs". Two enamoured people rejoice in having rediscovered that lost paradise.

> How beautiful are your feet in sandals.
> The curve of your thighs is like the work of an artist.
> Your breasts are like twin deers, like two gazelles.
> Your neck is like a tower of ivory. Solomon 7:14

#16 Ezechiel

A relief sculpture based on a detail of Michelangelo on the ceiling of the Sistine Chapel

#17 The Annunciation

The New Testament

#18

The Ottawa parish of the Annunciation commissioned me to do a sculpture fro their church to commemorate their 25th anniversary in 2010.

First I made two models, and the parish close the one of photo #17. So, during the cost and wet summer of 2009, I carved the 8 foot tall sculpture in my lean-to garage as shown in #19.

#19

#20 Big Christmas Sculpture

The Woodsource on Roger Stevens Drive laminated knot-free white pine into a 96" x69" for me to carve the Annunciation of #19. I turned the largest cut-off, above the wings and halo of the angel, into ths Christmas sculpture that encompasses all the Nativity events.

#21

The Christmas story never grows old. We ask questions today which would not have been asked in the Middle Ages: What census took place in Bethlehem at Jesus' birth? Was he really born in a stable? How much truly happened and how much is folk tale? But the essential joy of Christmas lasts: the revelation that life really matters, that our human lives have purpose, and that the love of God passionately pursues us.

Did the first Disciples of Christ recount snatches of his birth and youth around the evening cooking fire? It makes sense that, thanks to the need of recording the story of his martyrdom and redemption, the first Christians began to ask questions about his earlier life as well.

The same thing had happened with Hebrew Scriptures. During the seventy years of Babylonian captivity, the essential drama of the liberation from Egyptian captivity was embellished with Yahweh's general care starting with creation and on through the wanderings of the patriarchs. By way of storytelling, these humble beginnings were tacked on.

The same with the Jesus cult. And the more it moved north into Europe, the more it turned into a feast of light and dark, winter solstice, candles, Christmas trees, gift-giving, carolling, Santa Claus, jungle bells and mistletoe.

We delight in these stories and say, "Merry Christmas!"

22

#22 Mary visiting her cousin Elizabeth who is pregnant with John the Baptist.

#23

Madonna dello crucifisso

Artists were invited to submit a sketch for the door of an ancient Basilico in Ravena (see #76, and to work out one detail in bronze.

My theme was the power of the cross, and this Madonna sculpture would be at the apex.

#24 Madonna

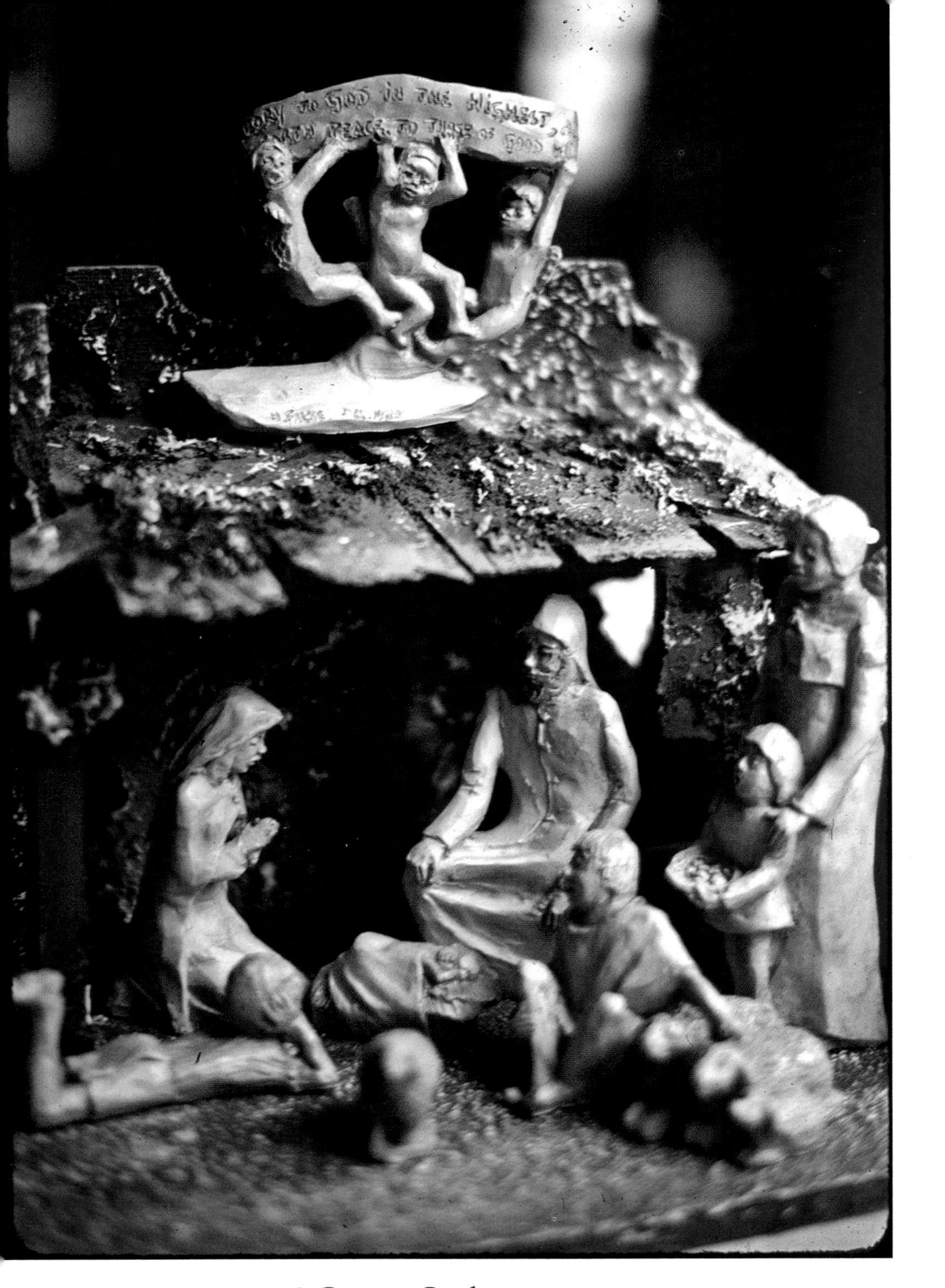

#25 Ceramic Creche

When around 1990 I was pastor of St. Joan of Arc in Toronto, Archbishop Ambrozic came for Confirmation. Just before the evening service I said to him, “if you want to change, use my room”. When a few minutes later he returned in his purple regalia, he said, “I saw your nice Nativity set. I would love to have it for my new residence.”

Two weeks later I delivered this set, after I had added three kings, a donkey and an ox. (He liked the sad donkey best of all.)

#26 A Ceramic of all of the Christmas Events

Fantasy of Mary nursing Jesus, while angels surround her singing praise to God.

#27

#28

#29

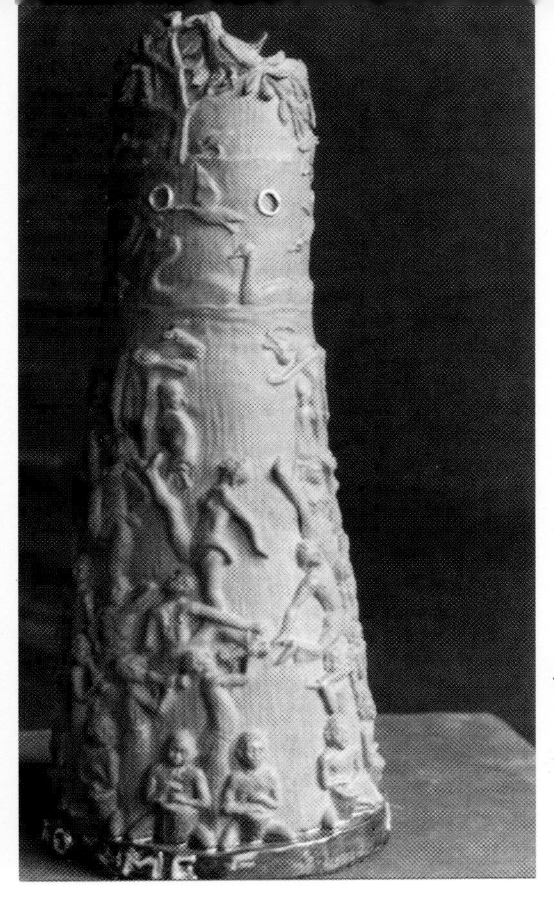

#30

#31

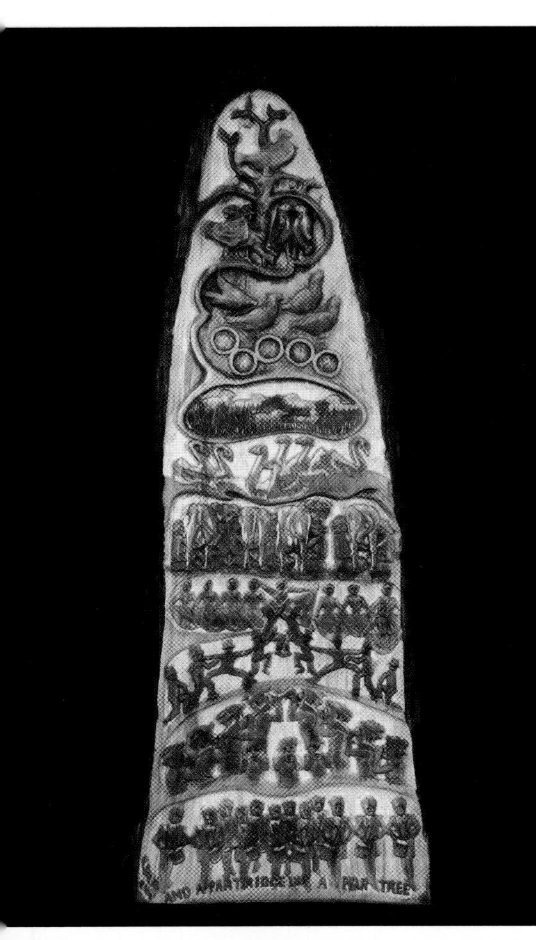

#32

The 12 days of Christmas

An ever-widening work space is needed to portray that Twelve Days, starting with a single partridge in a pear tree.

A hollow ceramic column is ideal, but even an expanding slab of cedar will do.

#33 Jesus teaching from Simon Peter's boat

Sermon on the Mount

The Sermon on the Mount, or the Beatitudes, provides a Christian vision of how we can make progress on our way to life with God forever.

It demands much more than just keeping the Ten Commandments, and it is certainly contrary to the mentality of the people who dominate public life and the economy. Those people have their own set of Beatitudes that go like this:

Blessed are those who are rich, for they control the wealth of the earth.

Blessed are those who forge ahead with their elbows, for they will build their careers.

Blessed are those who bend the laws to their advantage, for they will gain power.

Blessed are those who are impure of heart, for they can do whatever turns them on.

Blessed are those who wage war, for they will control the world.

Blessed are those who are without faith, without morality, for they can do whatever they want.

Such people of darkness will rule the earth as long as the children of light keep their mouths shut and do nothing.

#34

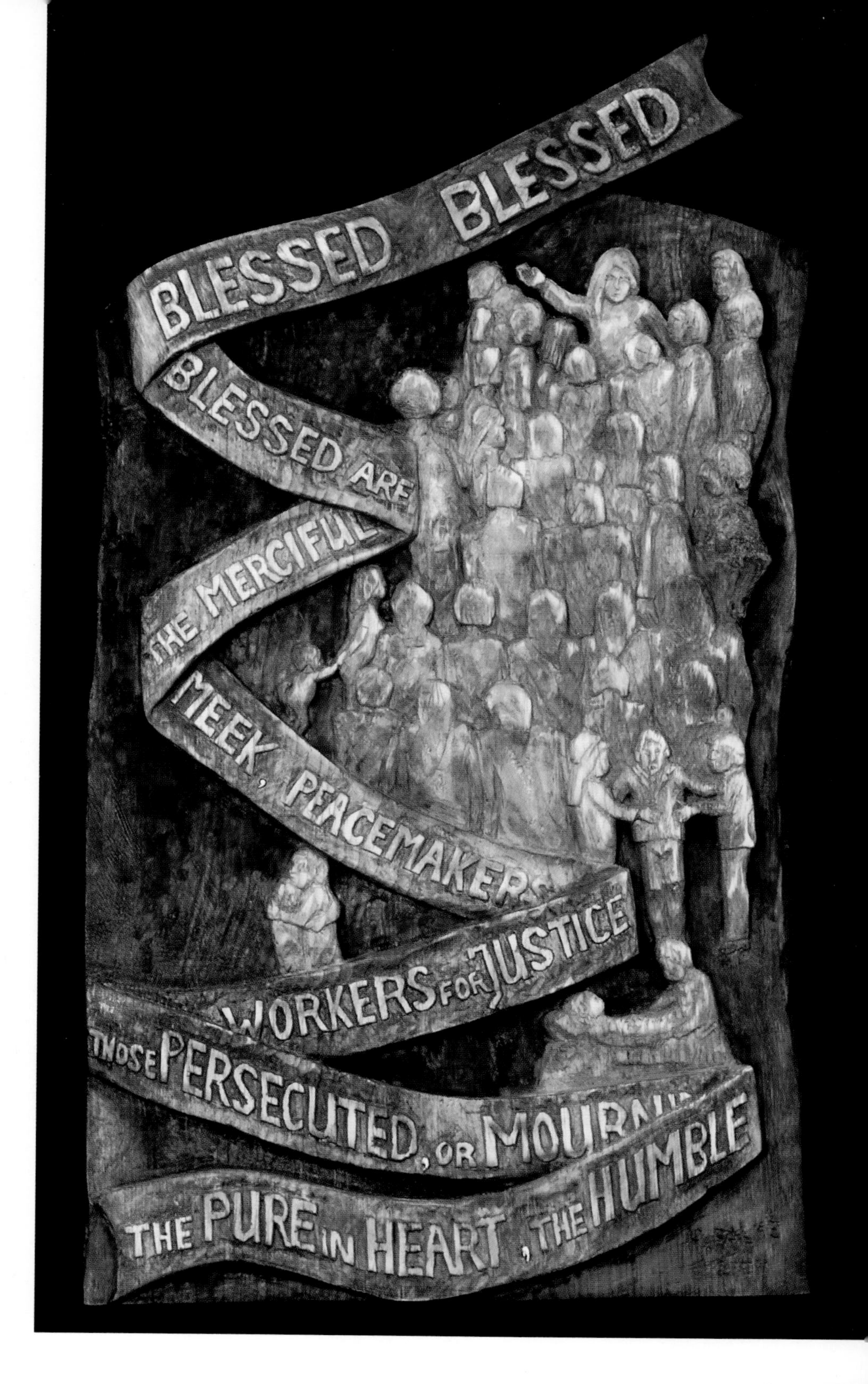
BLESSED BLESSED
BLESSED
BLESSED ARE
THE MERCIFUL
MEEK, PEACEMAKERS
WORKERS FOR JUSTICE
THOSE PERSECUTED, OR
THE PURE IN HEART, THE HUMBLE

#35 Lazarus

The parable of the rich man and Lazarus (Luke 1 6:19-31) illustrates that wealth is often a false front with little humanness behind it, while hidden behind poverty there may be a lovable person.

The poor in our society are literally downtrodden. People feel free to step on them, exploit them and use them for their own benefit.

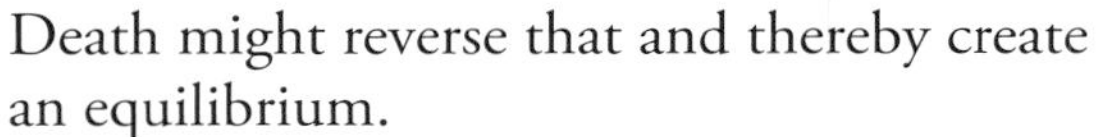

Death might reverse that and thereby create an equilibrium.

When I modelled the ceramic sketch in 1990, I had precisely that message in mind, although I had also other applications at heart: painters, sculptors, poets are often subject to ridicule and rejection. Even their private lives are fully investigated: bare bottom. Sometimes they will only overcome that after their death, when their worth is posthumously recognized. The large sculpture is a more abstract elaboration of the same parable.

#36

#37

#38 The Good Shepherd

The Pre-Raphaelite painter W.H. Hunt painted in 1852 a work called "Our English Coasts (Strayed Sheep)".

These "strayed sheep" were intended to illustrate the inadequacy of volunteer soldiers against a potential French invasion of England. It became, of course, easy in later years to give the painting a Christian connotation.

I blatantly obliged by introducing at the lower left a shepherd who brings up from the steep ravine a lost sheep.

#39 Zacchaeus, come down

Only a few years ago an economic report in the USA suggested that America should actively promote war. Weapons industry would create huge employment so that the US economy would quickly recover.

Fortunately, the US Bishops' Conference has rarely been more vocal in their protests.

The message of the Beatitudes is clear: those rooted in gentleness and righteousness will blossom forth into the Kingdom of God.

#40

From the parable: the prodical son feeding with the pigs.

#41

#42

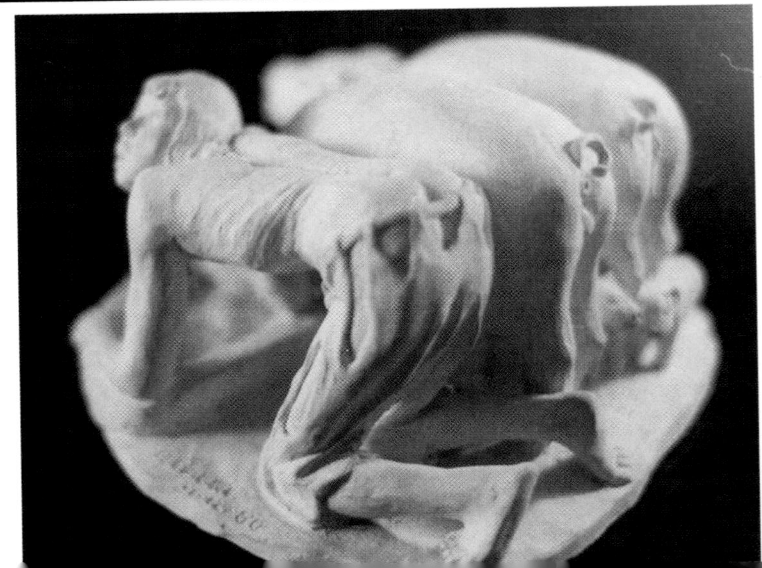

#43 Prodical Son and Forgiving Father

'The parable of the Prodigal Son is one of the best known stories of the Bible. It is only when he has arrived at the lowest point of his human dignity (like a die-hard alcoholic) that he comes to his senses.

However, there is so much more to this story.

That son is an ambiguous fellow. He is not really repentant of any of his major failures. He is just happy-go-lucky till he is facing the wall.

Actually, the parable is mainly about the father.

The point of the parable is not that God forgives us in spite of our worthlessness, but rather that no matter how sinful and worthless we are, there is still enough basic goodness and potential in us for God to love us.

This becomes even more obvious with the end of the parable. There is that other son who represents our traditional view of God as the great accountant in the sky who carefully tots up the assets and liabilities of our lives, and who might even allow us to bargain with him and present a list of good works to earn his forgiveness.

But a God who acts like the loving father who forgives us and embraces us even before we have had a chance to finish confessing our guilt, is too good to be true and actually unfit for our modern times.

The parable is one more illustration of Jesus' main teaching, which is the great patience and mercy of the Father, who simply refused to cut down the unfruitful tree because he hoped that next year it would bear fruit, especially when tended with loving care.

#44 The Parable of the Ten Bridesmaids

Jesus is telling this parable to illustrate the need for vigilance for one's spiritual well-being at all times.

If you are not vigilant and do not do what should be done, then you may miss the boat, and you will be excluded from the feast.

I have sculpted this parable in various ways.

In the small bronze medallion, the five lackadaisical bridesmaids are locked out, while the five wise ones clap their hands and shake their timbrels inside the compound.

The gray clay one with the semi-circular wall suggests that the broad way leads down to a dead end while the more challenging ascending path leads to flight on high.

A feminist nun asked me, "What are you working on these days?" I said, "The Five Foolish Bridesmaids." She came to look at it and then asked, "Where are the five wise ones?" I teased her by answering, "Are there any?"

#45

#46

#47 Woman at the Well

More often than not, I do several versions of a theme that captivates me. Jesus talking to the Samaritan woman at the well is a prime example.

The light-coloured one at the top was the first one I modelled. But then I felt the woman was a bit too dominant.

The second ceramic with the wooden backdrop was an improvement, although here Christ was too dominant and lecturing down to her.

The third one in butternut struck the right balance, I think.

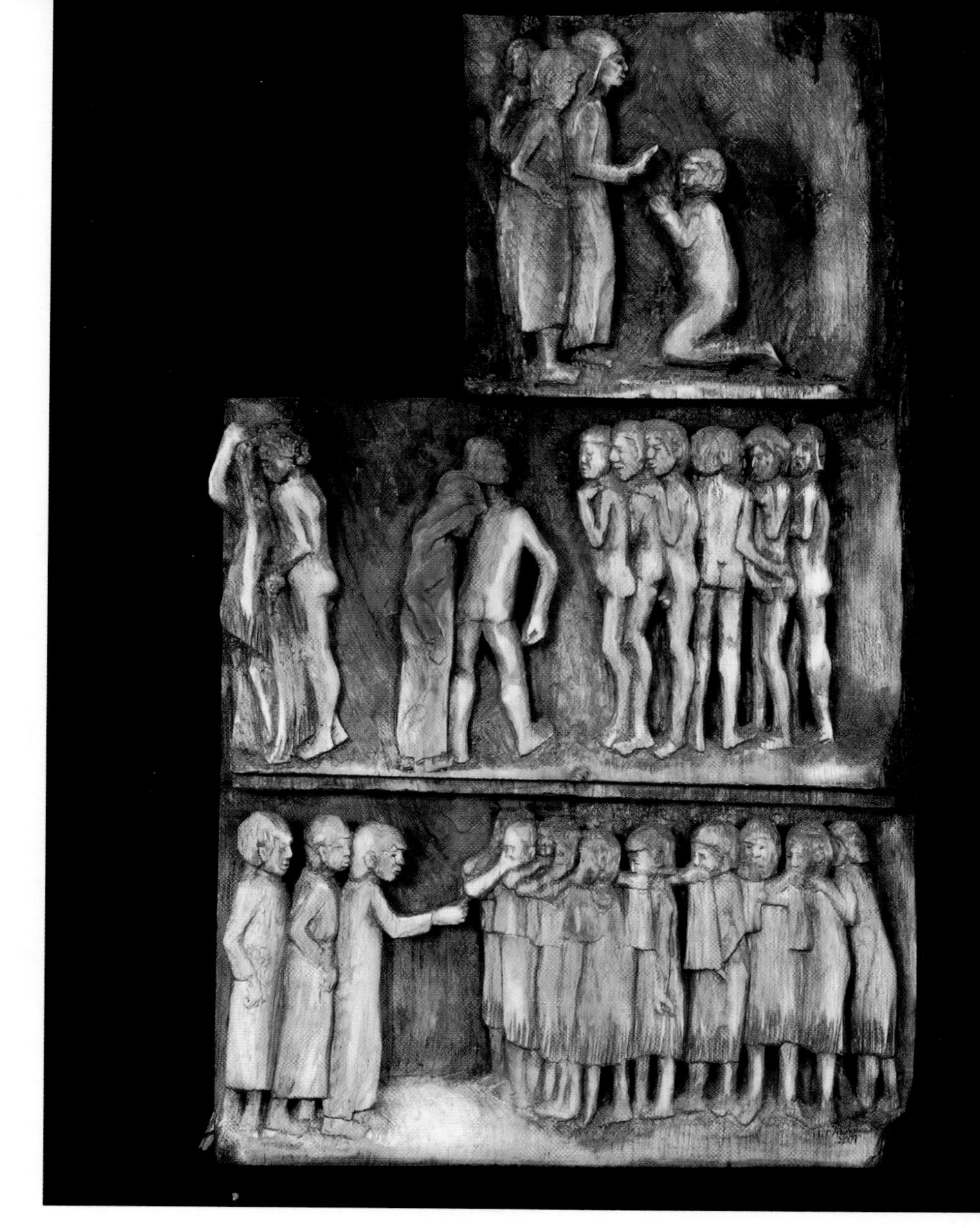

#48 Ten Lepers Cured

So true to life! People who have been seriously ill react the same. Returning home, many quickly forget the misery they went through and carry on with life as if nothing ever happened. A few have come to the realization that health is not to be taken for granted, and that life is a precious gift.

Of the ten lepers cured, nine quickly forget. However, the one who happened to be a Samaritan – a half-pagan, has been really touched by Jesus. All the others were cured, but this one is truly saved.

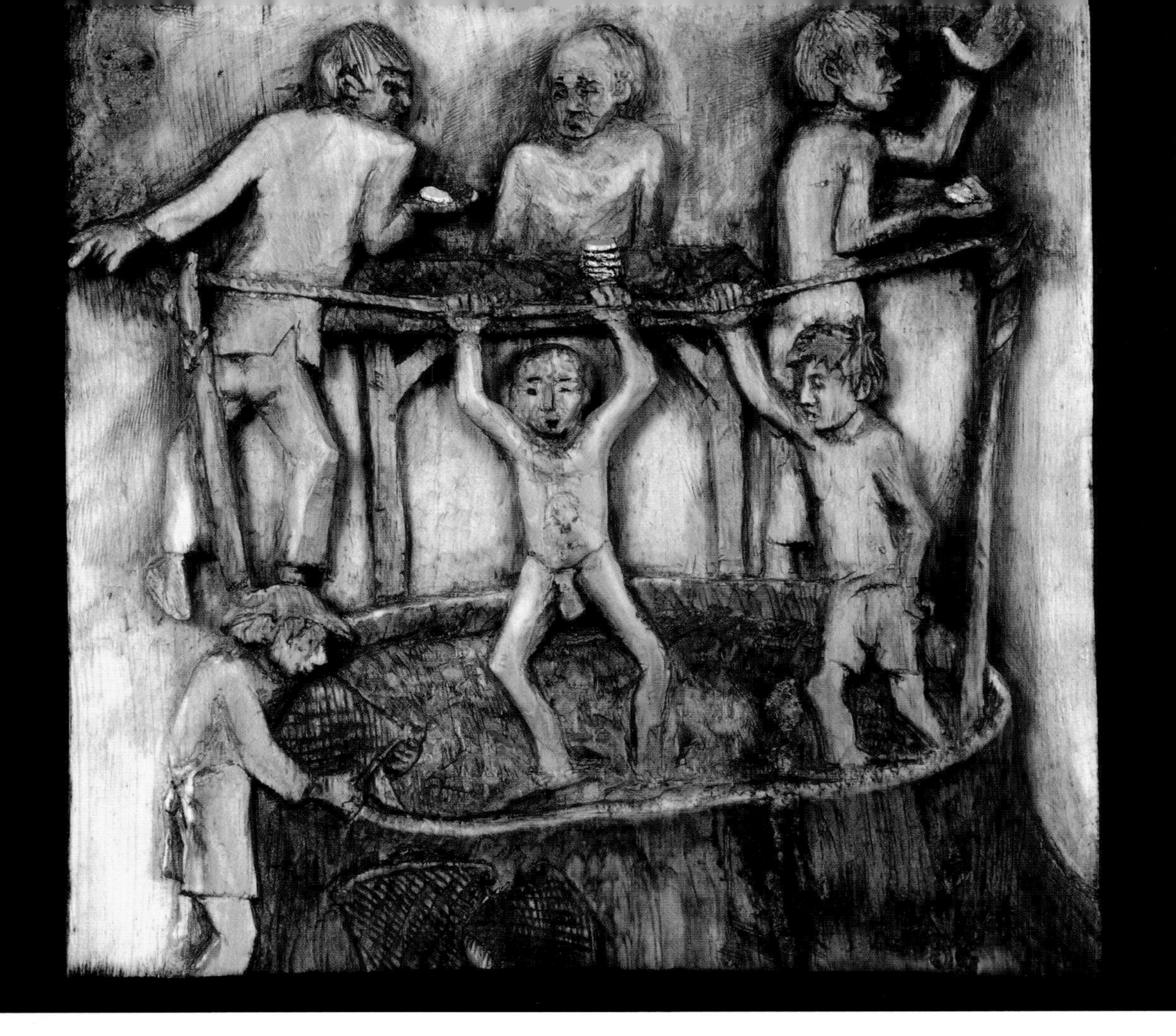

#49 Workers of the Last Hour

Day labourers work for minimum wages, and their jobs are insecure. While boys are already crushing the grapes with their feet, the owner has started to pay out wages. One who was hired last, walks away happy with full day's wages, while the man who was hired first receives the same full wages but grumbles, "that's not fair!"

Just so, God rewards all people who have worked according to their capabilities, with the same eternal life.

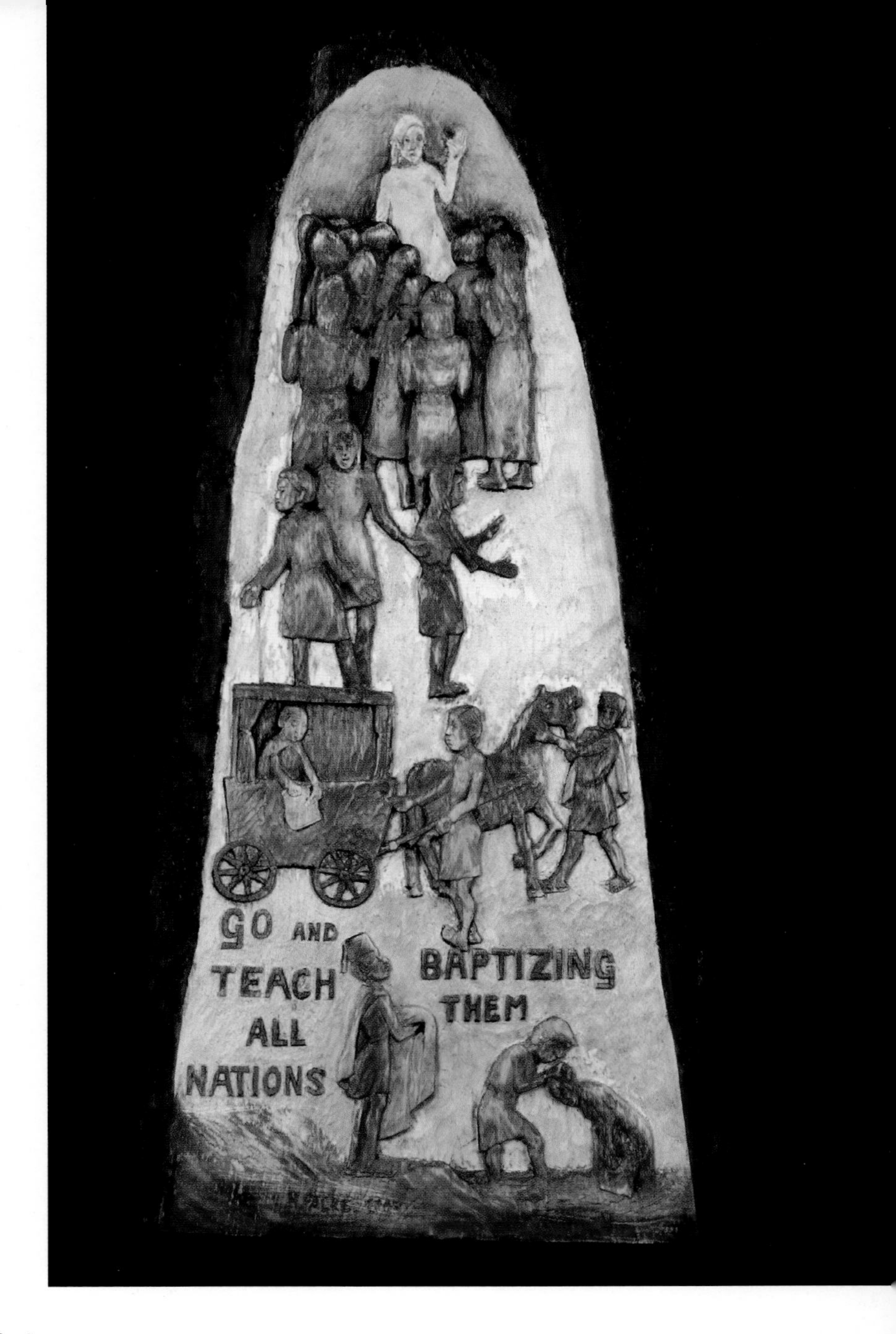

#50 Go and Teach All Nations

The Church has followed up this Great Mandate till just about every corner of the globe has been touched by it.

Acts 8:26-40 has a specific example from the very first days of Christianity.

A prominent Ethiopian on his journey home from Jerusalem runs into the Apostle Philip who instructs him and baptizes him along the road.

#51 Jesus riding a donkey on "Palm Sunday"

#52 Good Samaritan loading donkey

The Bible has several favourite animals: the dove as symbol of the Holy Spirit; the lamb as image of Christ, the Lamb of God.

Dogs and pigs are shunned as unclean animals.

The snake as symbol of cunning is also despised.

Even the horse is distrusted as it was mainly employed for war.

However, the Bible seems to have a place of honour for the donkey, the beast of burden for ordinary people.

Mary and Joseph travelled with a donkey, and when the good Samaritan bent down over the wounded Jew, the donkey waited patiently to serve as an ambulance for the victim.

Jesus chose the donkey for his solemn entrance into Jerusalem on Palm Sunday. The prophet Zechariah foretold, "God will remove the war chariots from Israel and take the horses from Jerusalem; the bows used in battle will be destroyed. Shout for joy, you people of Jerusalem! Look, your king is coming to you humble and riding a donkey." (Zech 9.9-10).

#53 Detail, first of two slightly different versions of "The Good Samaritan

#54 Second version of "The Good Samaritan"

#55 A Celtic Cross

The Passion of Christ has become the instrument of our Redemption, and is therefore a major object of Christian creative art.

After a dozen complete sets of Stations of the Cross for Churches, the two sculptures on this page have in recent years become the most requested forms of crucifixes for me.

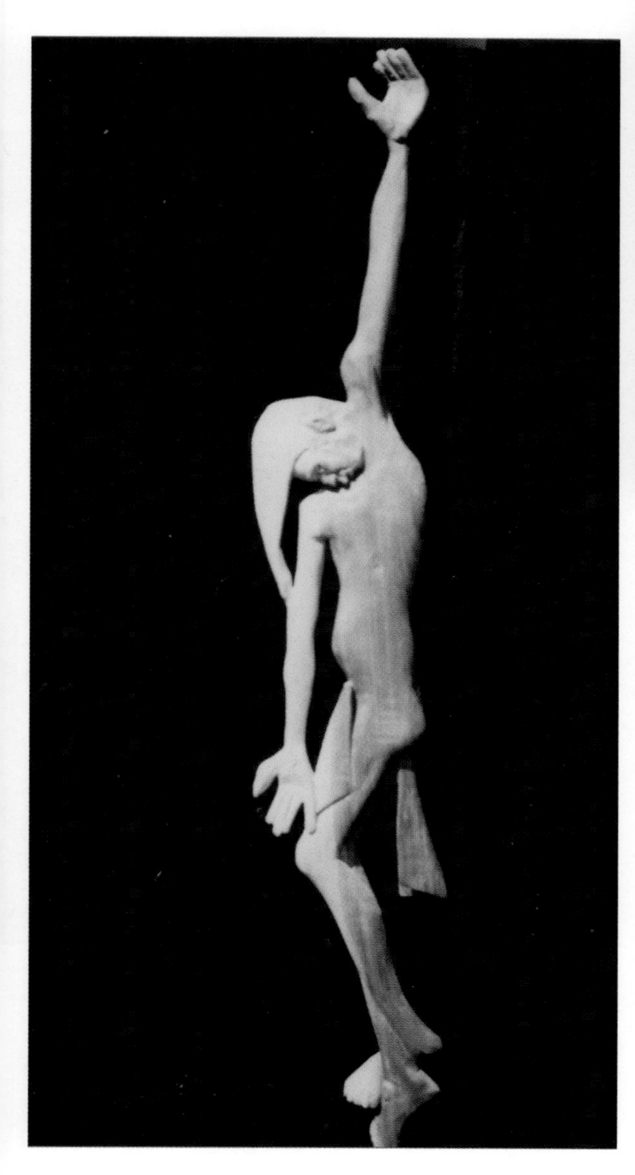

The Celtic Cross allows a great deal of freedom of expression. This one was requested for a family in Galway, Ireland. Hence the Cathedral of Galway at the bottom, and the shamrock opposite the maple leaf. All the other images are related to Easter and the events of the Emmaus disciples.

The other sculpture is actually my favourite Sacred Heart image under the title, "I've given all."

#56 I've Given All

#57 Last Supper

In the last supper of Leonardo Da Vinci, Jesus must have said something like, "Guys, if you want to be in the picture, sit at this side of the table."

In my Last Supper of the shared eyes, featured on the facing page, Jesus may have said, "Guys, I am the only one with 20-20 vision".

However, no doubt there were some tense, emotional moments during that farewell meal. Therefore, as the Roman numeral I at the right bottom indicates, this scene is the appropriate first Station of the Cross in modern up-dated Stations of the Cross.

#58 Last supper of the "shared eyes"

The Garden of Olives is the setting for the arrest of Jesus.

Judas the betrayer indicates Jesus while the apostles sneak away behind the olive trees.

When a soldier grabs the young man to the right, he escapes naked, leaving whatever he was wearing in the grasp of the soldier (Mk 14:50-52)

Tradition has it that the young man was Mark himself, the writer of the first gospel.

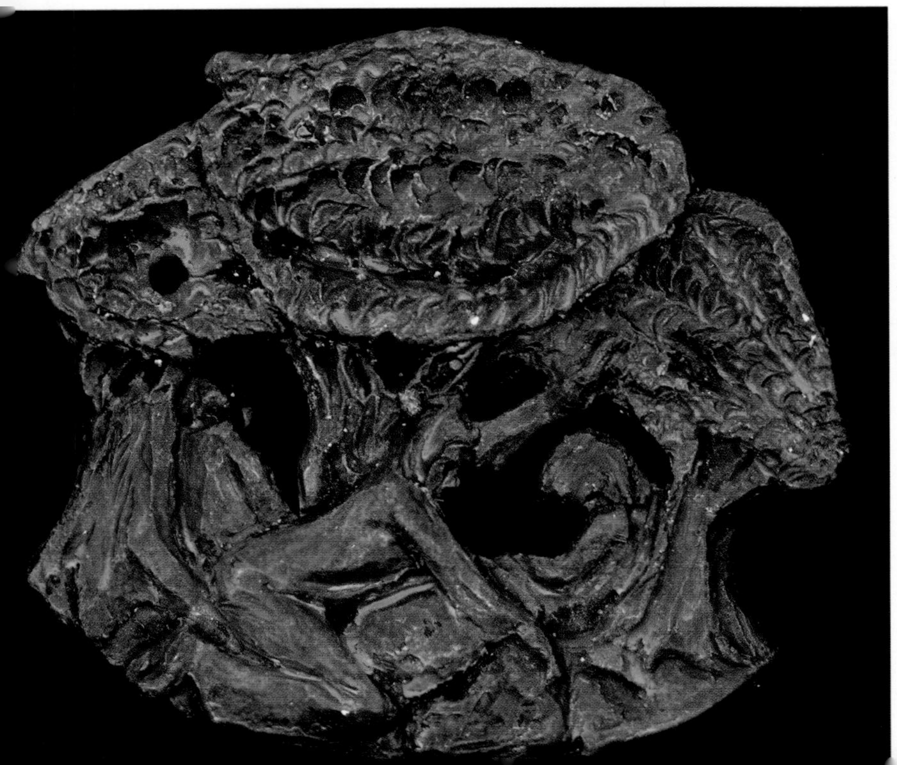

#59

#60 Long Sculpture of the Garden of Olives

The Garden of Olives is the setting for the arrest of Jesus.

Judas the betrayer indicates Jesus while the apostles sneak away behind the olive trees.

When a soldier grabs the young man to the right, he escapes naked, leaving whatever he was wearing in the grasp of the soldier (Mk 14:50-52)

Tradition has it that the young man was Mark himself, the writer of the first gospel.

#61 Jesus' agony

Mt 26:27 states, "Sadness came over him and great distress, then he said to the three apostles, 'my soul is sourrowful to the point of death' as he foresaw his horrible execution on Calvary.

#62 Sacrificial Victims

During my six years of teaching Fine Arts in a Ugandan College, I came across a fascinating custom in the near past. Men who had dared to express opposition to the ruling despot of the Baganda would at his nod be summarily stripped and chained to each other to be thrown and fed to the crocodiles. But before their legs would be broken, the victims were encouraged or even forced to drug themselves with a strong drink, so that their ghosts would not haunt the ruling despot.

#63

#64

Sacrificial Victims (continued)

Christ is of course our supreme example of sacrificial victim. Sacred Scriptures refer to him as the Lamb of God led to be slaughtered.

To appease the Jewish leaders, Pilate condemned Jesus to the Roman death of common criminals, i.e. a bloody scourging to break their bodily strength before their crucifixion. Jesus must have been horribly aware that as soon as he would be immobilized against the whipping pillar, his body would be quickly turned into carrion for the wild dogs, the crows, and the swarms of bottleflies and wasps on Calvary.

Up into our own age, individuals have been sacrificed for political reasons.

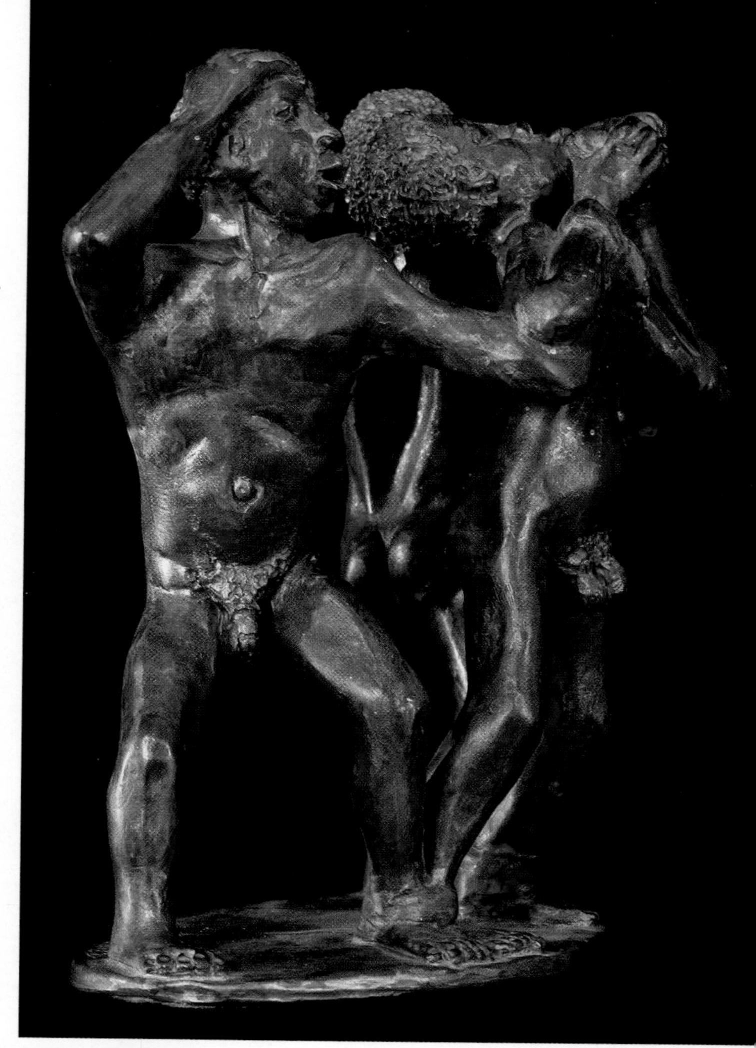

#65

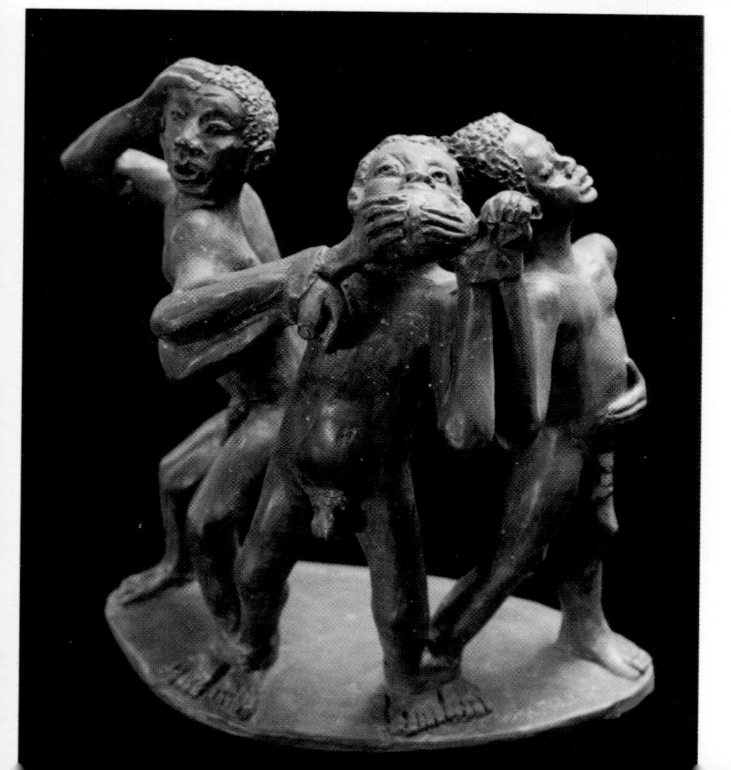

#66 Joan of Arc, the Maiden of Orleans, to be burned at the stake

#67 Jesus condemned by Pilate

Crucifixion:

Each year, hundreds of criminals were crucified on Calvary, sometimes two to a pole. It was a popular spectacle to see these robust victims writhe and agonize. And only one skeleton of a crucified person was ever found.

To be crucified meant to be totally destroyed; nothing should be left over. Animals would get the flesh; bones would be dumped in lime kilns.

Clothing was eagerly sought by the executioners by way of a tip.

Humiliation was intended, and the victims were usually naked: they had lost all rights to dignity and privacy. Still we can understand why most Christians find it uncomfortable to look at a naked Christ crucified. "He became like us in everything except sin." But we prefer to create an artificial exception here. My crucifixes are intended to make people uncomfortable for a moment of personal reflection on how unconditional Jesus' love for us was.

#68 Ecce Homo

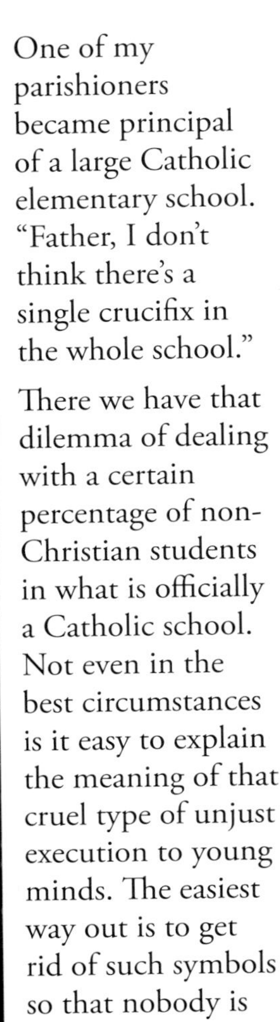

#69

One of my parishioners became principal of a large Catholic elementary school. “Father, I don’t think there’s a single crucifix in the whole school.”

There we have that dilemma of dealing with a certain percentage of non-Christian students in what is officially a Catholic school. Not even in the best circumstances is it easy to explain the meaning of that cruel type of unjust execution to young minds. The easiest way out is to get rid of such symbols so that nobody is offended.

“Father, could you make for us a crucifix that is not oppressive or sad, but, say, suggesting the Resurrection?”

I made three ceramic models, one of which would have to be duplicated 40 times.

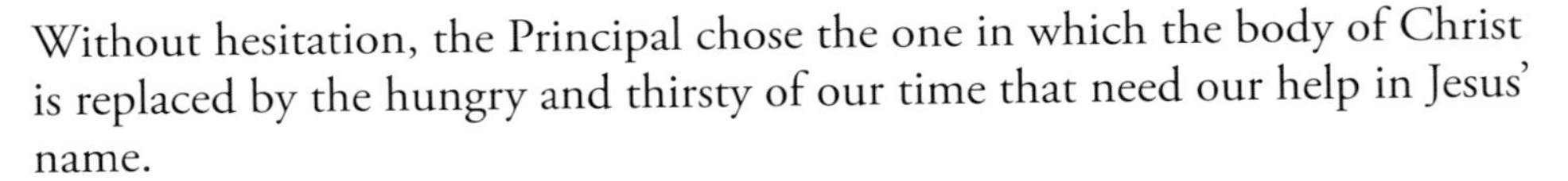

Without hesitation, the Principal chose the one in which the body of Christ is replaced by the hungry and thirsty of our time that need our help in Jesus’ name.

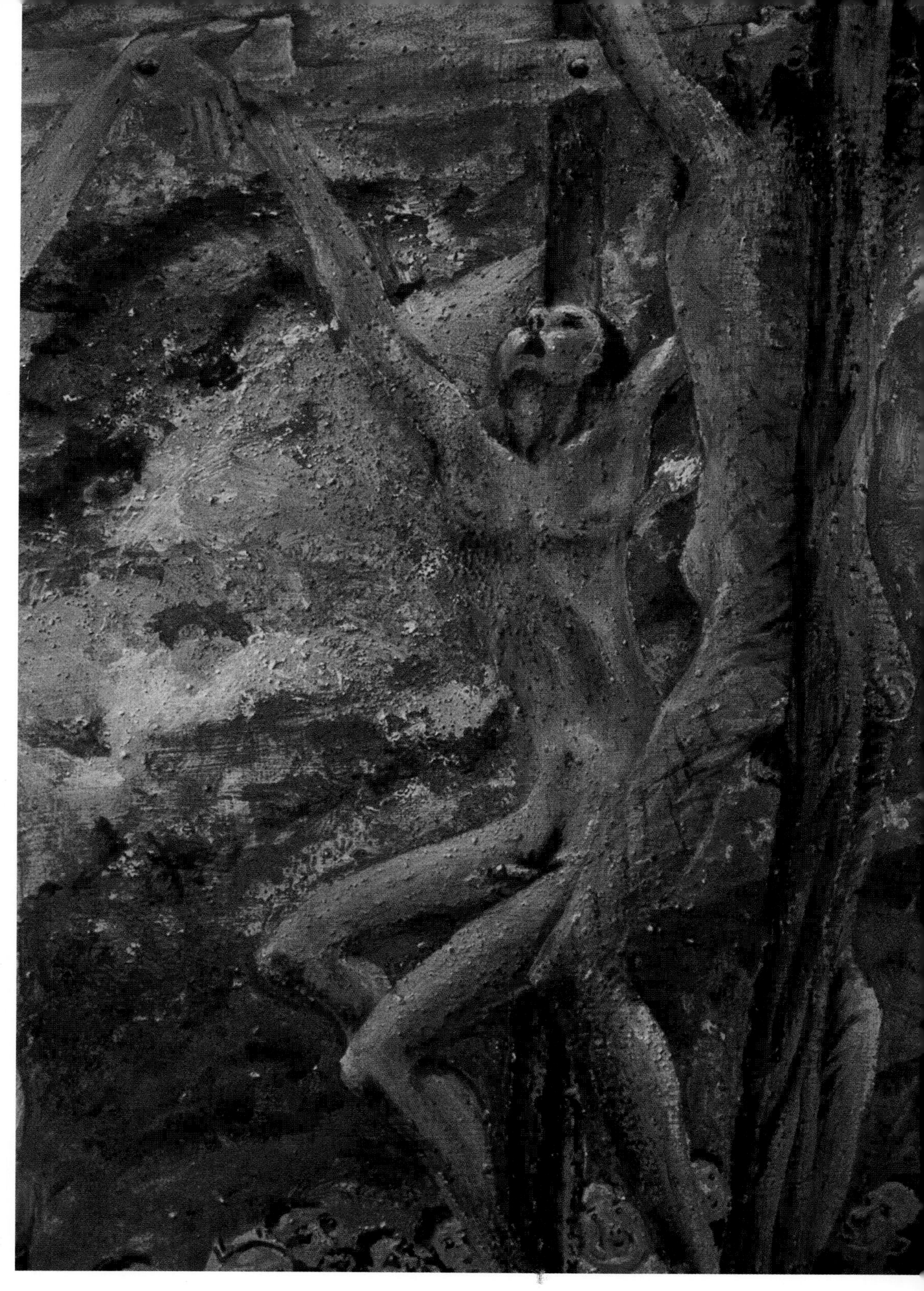

#70 Crucified

"At noon the whole country was covered with darkness, which lasted for three hours." Mt 27:45

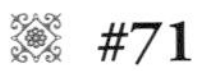 **#71**

Dividing the clothing, but gambling for the better pieces.

#72

#73 Crucified

#74 Pieta

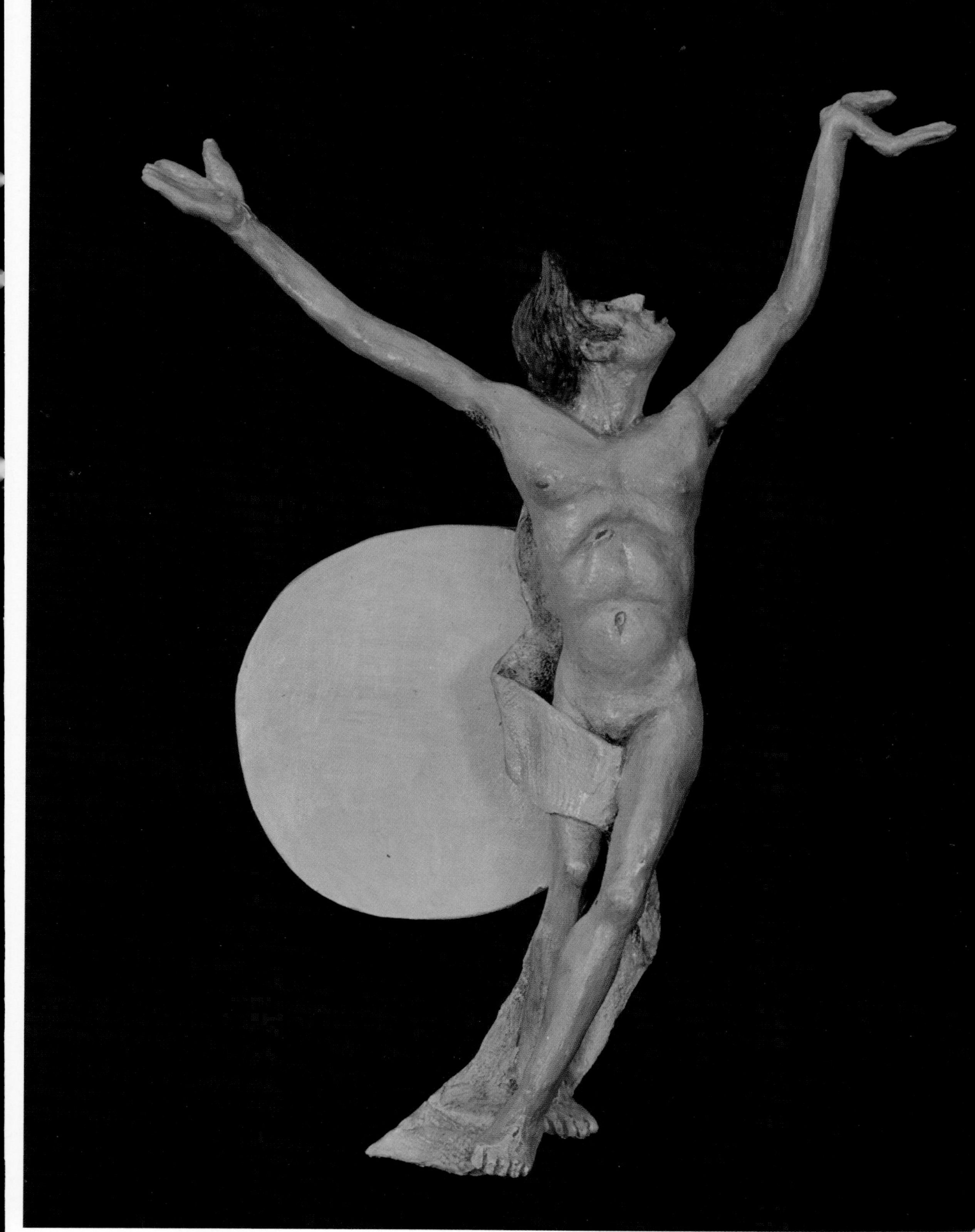

#75 Resurrection Ascension

#76 Sketch for Door of Basilica, Ravenna

#77 Basilica of St. Francis, Ravenna near Venice, Northern Italy

A series of 16 biennales have been held to build up a Dante Museum in Ravenna, in an old Franciscan Monastery where Dante happens to be buried. In 1990 I participated for the first time and was asked to become a member of the international jury for judging the more than 300 entries each second summer. Each time a specific theme related to Dante was given beforehand to all possible participants.

During the last Biennale in 2002, it was proposed that the theme for the next one in 2004 would be a sketch for the actual massive door of the old St. Francis Basilica in Ravenna. Apart from the sketch, each artist could work out one small detail in bronze.

Not knowing that there would be no next Biennale, I worked out my sketch: my theme was the power of the cross.

- At the top is the "Madonna della Crucifisso" which I also worked out in a small bronze sculpture (#23).
- Below that is St. Francis receiving the stigmata from the crucifix, as is described in Dante's Paradiso.
- Next is the scene on Calvary, and Jesus' compassion on the "Good Thief"
- Below that is a scene from Dante's Purgatorio where people are writhing on trees.
- At the bottom is a scene from Dante's Inferno, where Annas and Caiphas and other leaders who brought about Jesus' crucifixion, are themselves crucified naked and tossed to where people have to step over them.
- Along the edge are ten saints who are featured in Dante's three books.

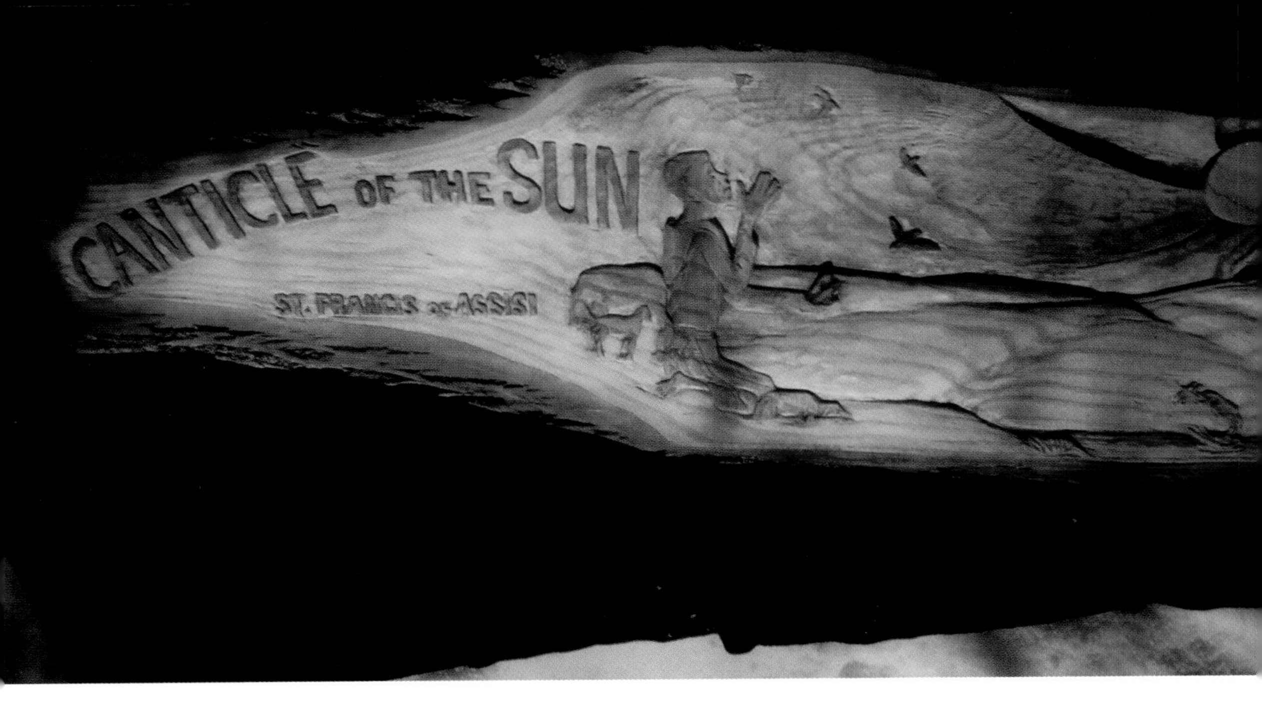

#78 Two halves of St Francis' "Canticle of the Sun"

Francis lived in the 13th century, son of a rich cloth merchant. He liked dancing, singing, and fighting. In one of those fights against a neighbouring town he got severely wounded. During his long convalescence he came to his senses, broke with his father, and even stripped naked to return his rich clothes to him, saying: "From now on, I'll have nothing to do with your world of money and power; I only call God in heaven my father."

At the start of his conversion he withdrew to the forested mountains above Assisi where he lived among the rejects of society: robbers, lepers, vagabonds, and animals. There he learned to love all creation and to live with nature and animals.

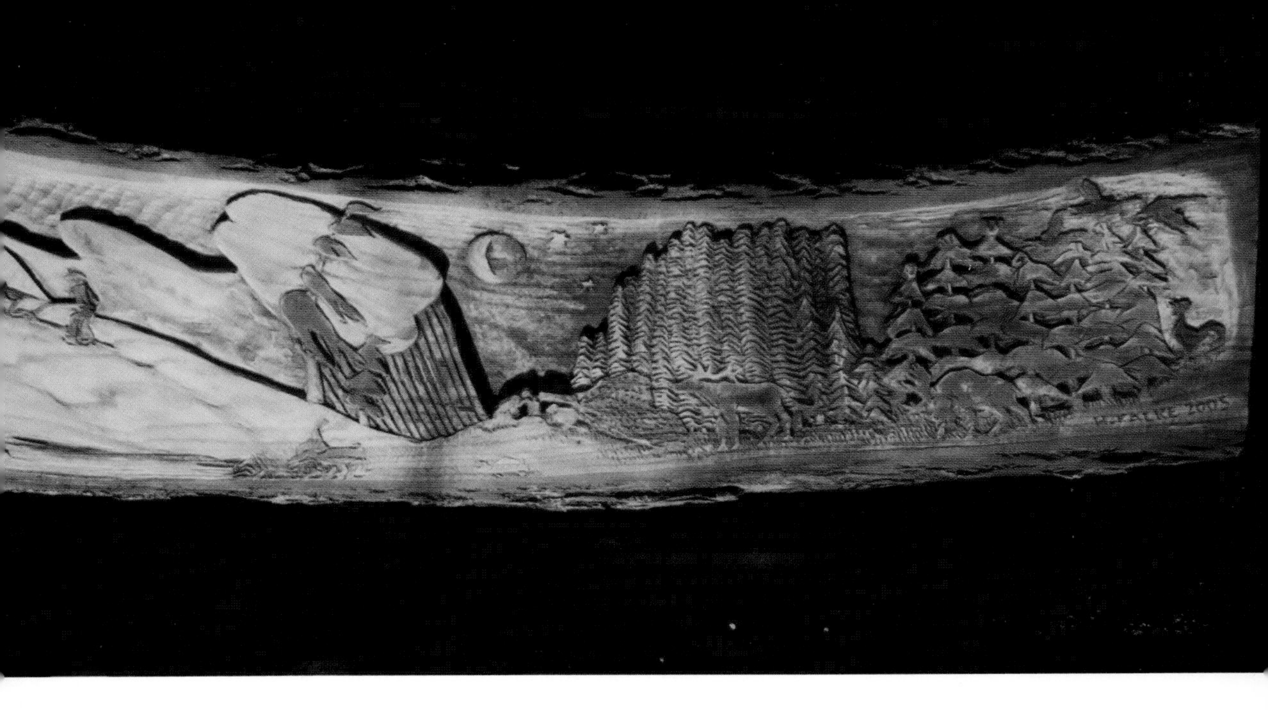

#79 St Francis

#80 Mural of St. Francis Canticle of the Sun

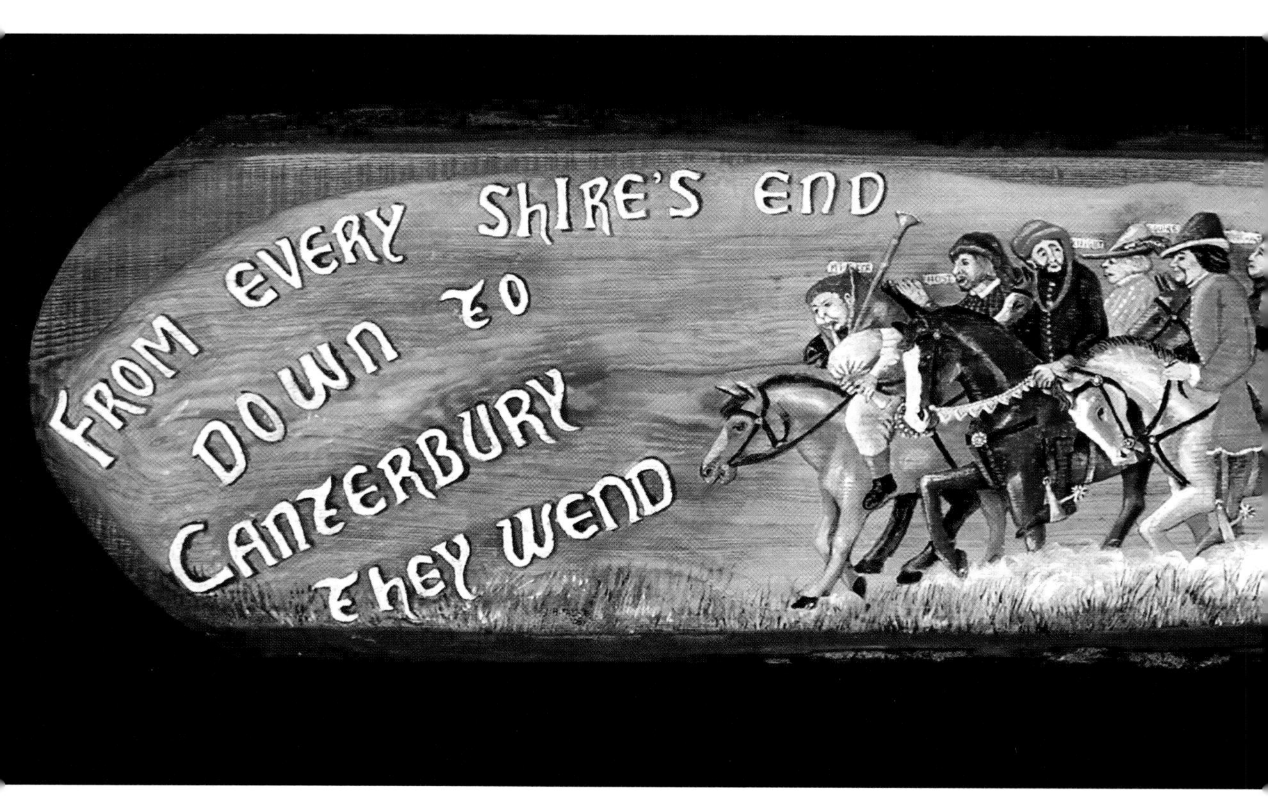

I converted an old engraving into a detailed painted relief scupture of all Chaucer's characters.

#81 Canterbury pilgrims

The Human Landscape

Throughout the years 2008 & 2009 I continued the series of "human landscapes" that were featured in my last publication "Sculpted Swan Songs", p. 88-109. The 39 works shown here are now continued with 38 new ones. To the Quebec painters of rural homesteads and villages, Krieghoff, Gagnon, Horik and Tex Lecor, I now add Louise Kirouac and Claude Langevin. They and several others have intrigued me so much that I borrow freely from their compositions for sculpted oval landscapes of my own.

Some adaptations are so free that the borrowing is almost unrecognizable. I will therefore often refrain from pointing out the borrowings, which to most people are pointless anyway.

#82 Roadside Crucifix, after Clarence Gagnon

#83 After Clarence Gagnon "Midnight Mass"

#84 Yellow Houses Baie St. Paul

#85 Combined from works of Paul Tex Lecor

#86

After four landscapes done by Vladimir Horik in Charlevoix County, northeast Quebec.

#87

#88

#89

#90

Freely composed after four Quebec village paintings done by Louise Kirouac

#91

#92

#93

#94

Three Charlevoix paintings done more closely after works by Vladimir Horik

#95

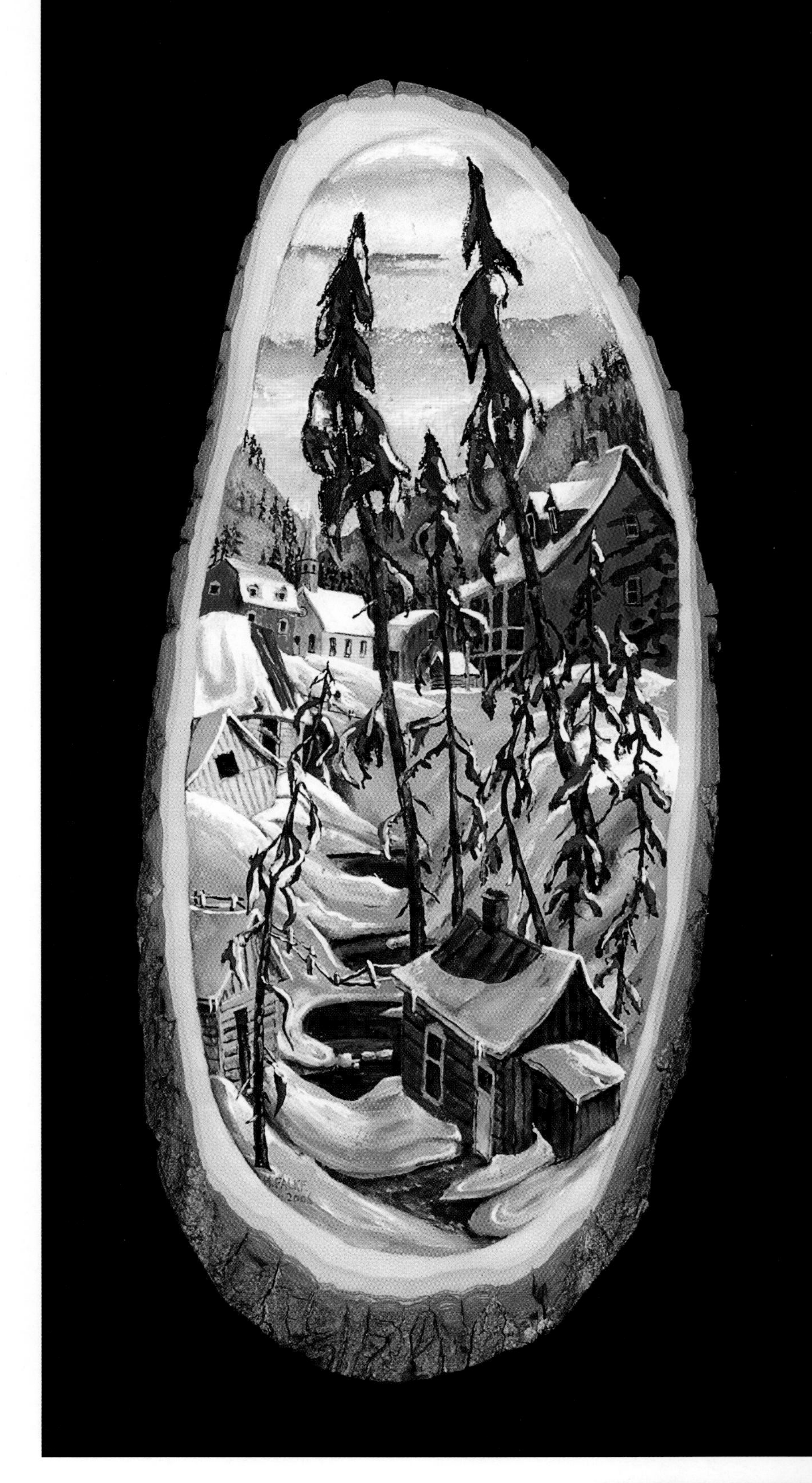

#96

#97

Three works inspired by paintings of Claude Langevin

#98 Snowdrifts

#99 The last cord of firewood

#100

Four paintings of Charlevoix County based on ink drawings or paintings by Vladimir Horik

#101

#102

#103

#104

Freely composed, but house and barn inspired by a work of Marcel Fecteau

#105 Harbour on the Gulf of St. Lawrence

#106 After "At Mass, Baie St. Paul" 1871-1953

#107 Entrance to Baie St. Paul

#108 Pacific Rim off Vancouver Island

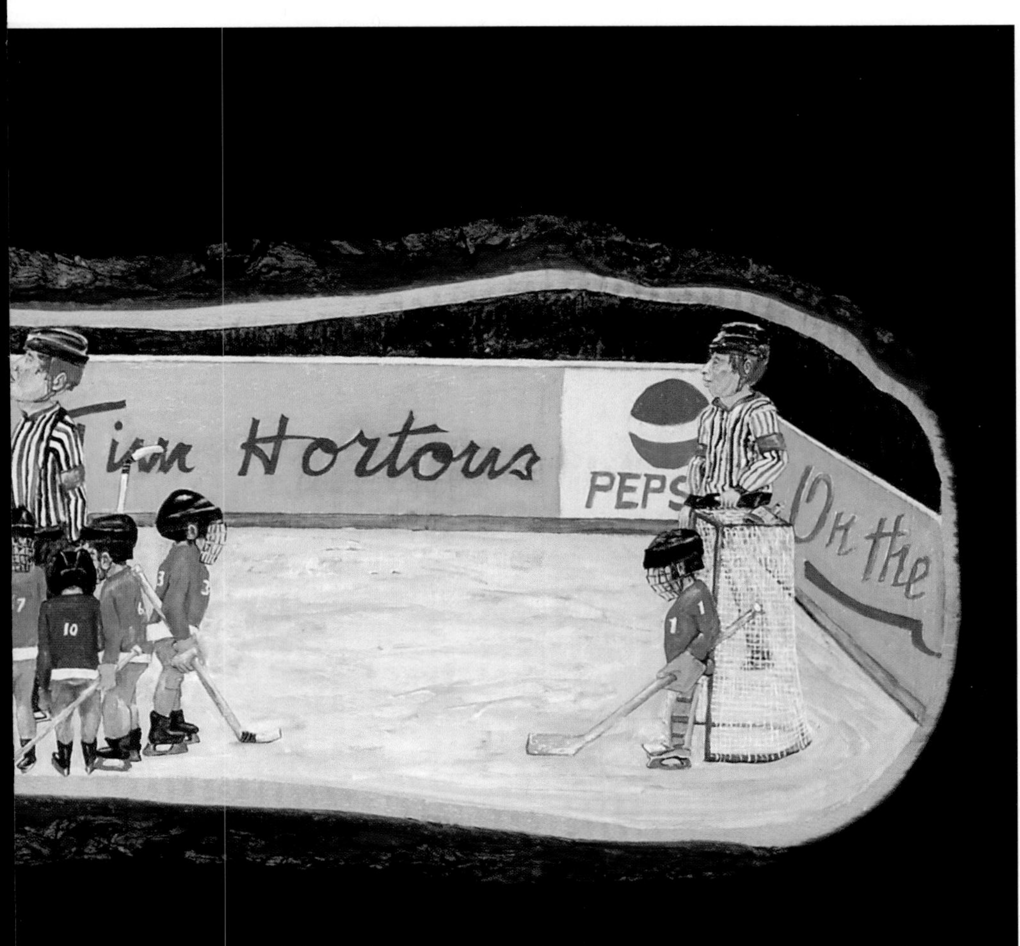

#109 Pee Wee Hockey brawl

#110

Two final inspirations from work of Vladimir Horik

#111

#112 Amsterdam by evening

Europe

Finally I have started to tap into sources for my "human landscapes" from the parts of Europe I am familiar with: Western Europe.

You will notice the obvious difference with inspirations derived from rural life in Quebec. Europe is crowded and often a quaint agglomeration of very ancient habitats.

#113 Old Bridge in Florence

#114 San Gimignano, Tuscany, land of Chianti wine and Lacrima Christi

#115 Venice

#116 The Herring Net

Winslow Homer (1836-1910) was a down-to-earth American painter who has nothing of those deceptive aesthetic frills and flourishes that the fashionable painters of his time, as well as their American imitators, were using. Small wonder that some contemporary critics, accustomed to pretty French Barbizon paintings like the sweet peasants of Millet and Corot, would call Homer's work damnably ugly. He composed his best works, not in order to present a colourful delight for the eyes, but in order to put across an idea and to honestly tell it as it is. "The Herring Net" shows the hard and dangerous work of deep-sea fisherman. No idealizing – just communicating ideas.

Homer was at home in the northern wilderness of Canada and the Adirondacks, and loved the drifting canoes and bobbing fishing boats off the coast of Maine where he lived. But he had no desire to romanticize the scenes, or think of them in terms of colour patterns, the way his contemporaries, the Impressionists and Fauves, did.

#117 Based on Emily Carr's paintings

#118 Fog Coming Up

Personal Creations

In the 1960s, when corrugated iron sheets became more desirable for roofing, I preferred making paintings of the traditional thatched huts, and I always invited some of the more ambitious Ugandan students to come and paint along with me; I was interested in teaching them the beauty of natural surfaces, and light versus shadow.

#119

The prophet Jeremiah lived in tough times, and the people were not very attentive to his lamentations and dire warnings of doom. No wonder Michelangelo painted him on the ceiling of the Sistine Chapel as deeply lost in thought.

This fourth and largest section is light-hearted and steps away from the meditative atmosphere of the bible sections. I hope you say to yourself, "Oh, he can be funny, too."

These "personal creations" are real gleanings, as the subtitle of the book suggests. They include humour, sensuality, nostalgia, and a bit of our history.

#120 At the edge of Zingha forest, Uganda

#121

Even the simplest hut of stickes, mud and grass can be colourful and attractive.

#122 Painted from our house on Daly Avenue, Ottawa after a typical December snowstorm

#123

#124

Upon being urged by Idi Amin in 1974 to leave Uganda, I continued the same search for "picturesque" natural buildings in the Ottawa area. The one above, in Carlsbad Springs, was left untouched, with furniture and cupboards inside, because grandmother was still living in sight of her old home. However, a bunch of horses had a free run of the place and destroyed the weakened wooden floor.

#125

#126

People of my parish in Pendleton saw my paintings at a local exhibition, and requested me to paint their properties

The first was a Mr. Shane who wanted me to do his sugar shack.

Then, another parishioner, Mr. Ryan, kept asking me to do a painting of his rather ordinary farm. When the family noticed that I paid attention to ordinary details like the mailbox, and the cow to the left that had just calved in the pasture, they kept chasing their horse in my view to the right. And behold, it was included.

H. FALKE 2008

Blume", The Rock", 1945-

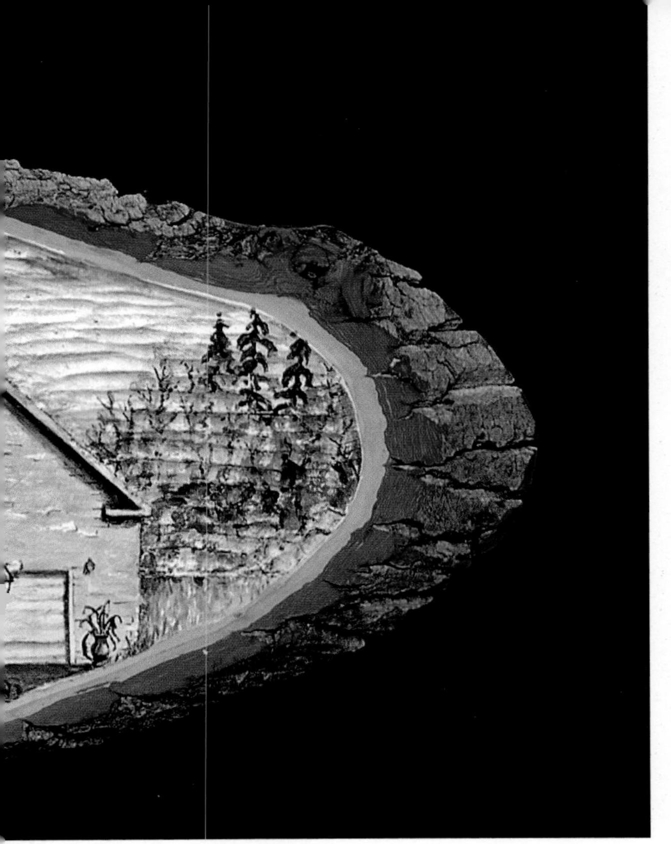

#127

Even as recent as 2009 I was persuaded by the Serafinis to do the home of their neighbours, The Haggars, as a wedding present. So I still did not put up the sign, "Dear Parishioners, I am not a house painter."

Frank Lloyd Wright built a famous dream-house over a running brook in Pennsylvania. While the construction was in full swing, as shown at the extreme left, the artist Blume made a fantasy painting of how the old ruins were making room for the modern structure.

Intentionally, my sculpture was done in one piece of cedar honouring the two creative artists together.

#128

Humourous Subject Matter

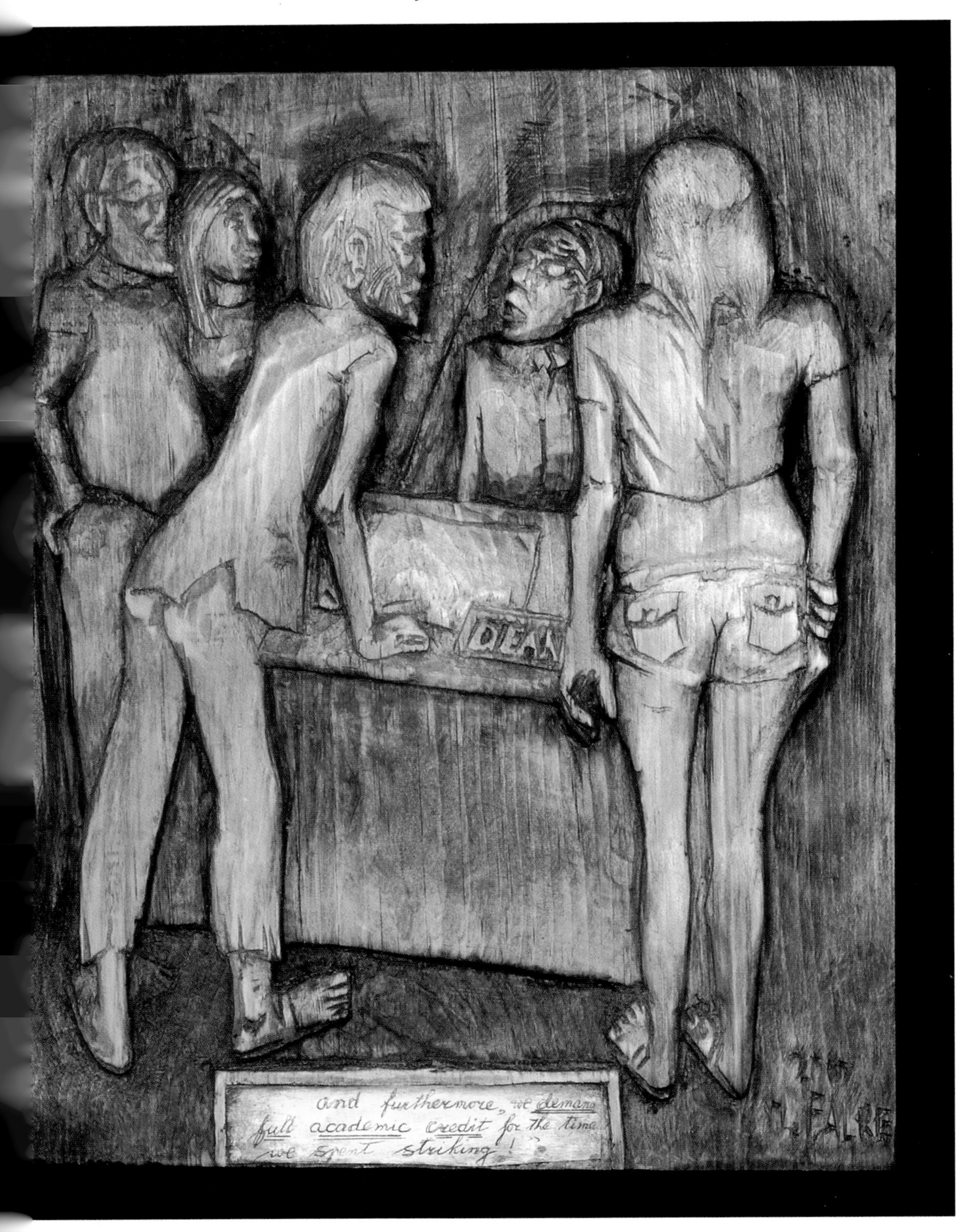

#129 Students settling strike with the Dean

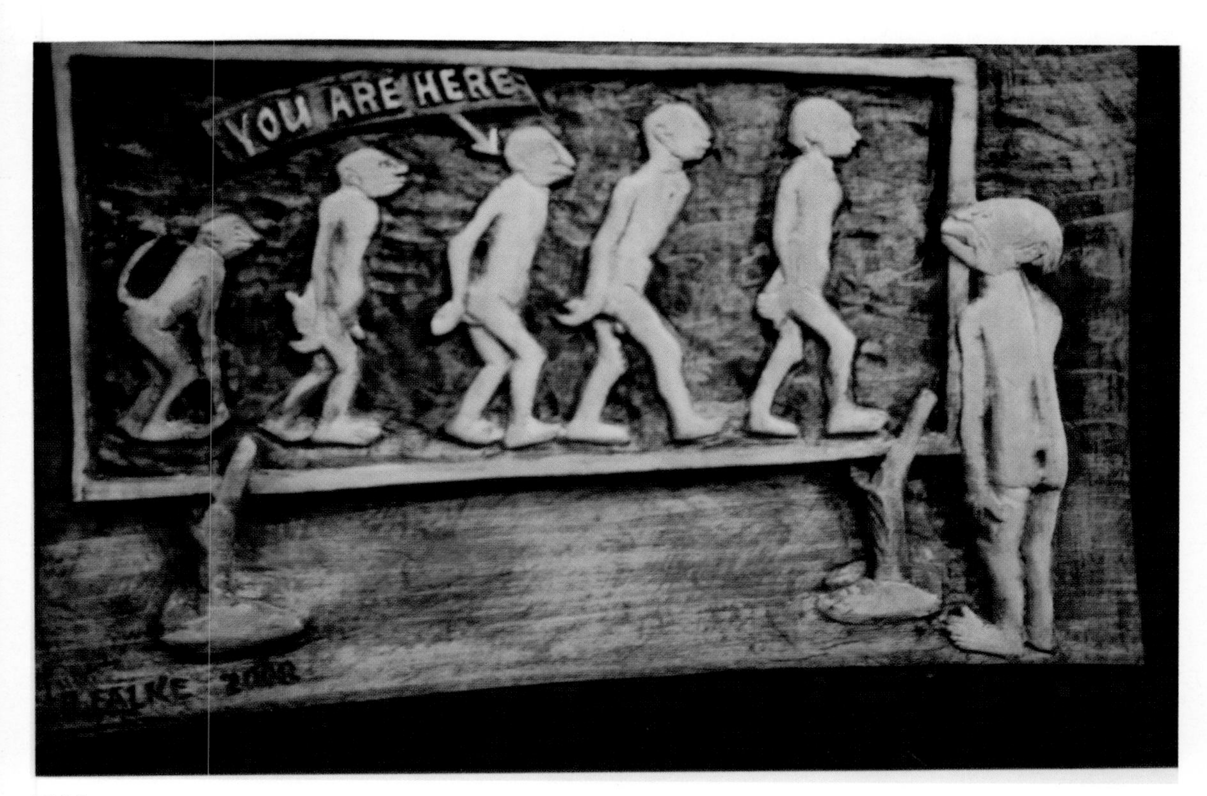

#130

#131
Inspired by
The Beatles

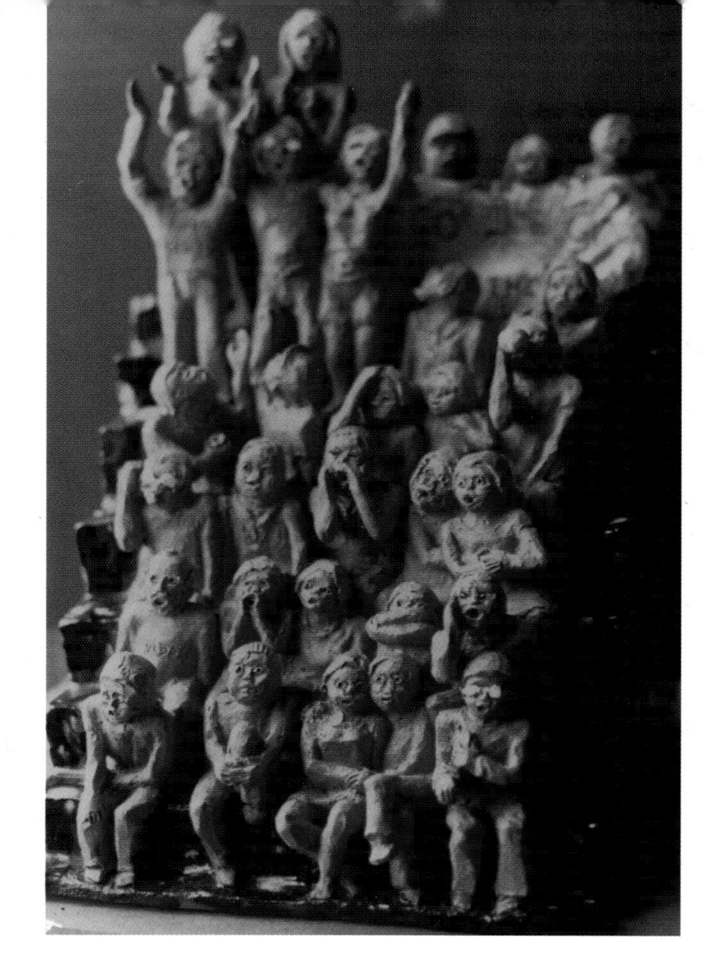

#132

Watching a football game.
Two versions.

#133

#134

#135

"They shouldn't look at that!"

At the subway escalator a recent immigrant can get confused.

#136

#137 Column of dancing through the centuries.

#138 Here's the twist of our time.

Sensuous subject matter

#139

Greek mythology tells of a beauty contest between the three Graces. The winner receives a golden apple.

I presented this fine stone sculpture at Immaculata High School graduation as the art prize for the year.

#140

#141 Leda and the Swan

#142 After a calendar photo promoting curling!

#143 Lute playing woman

**#143
Flying too
close to
the sun**

#144

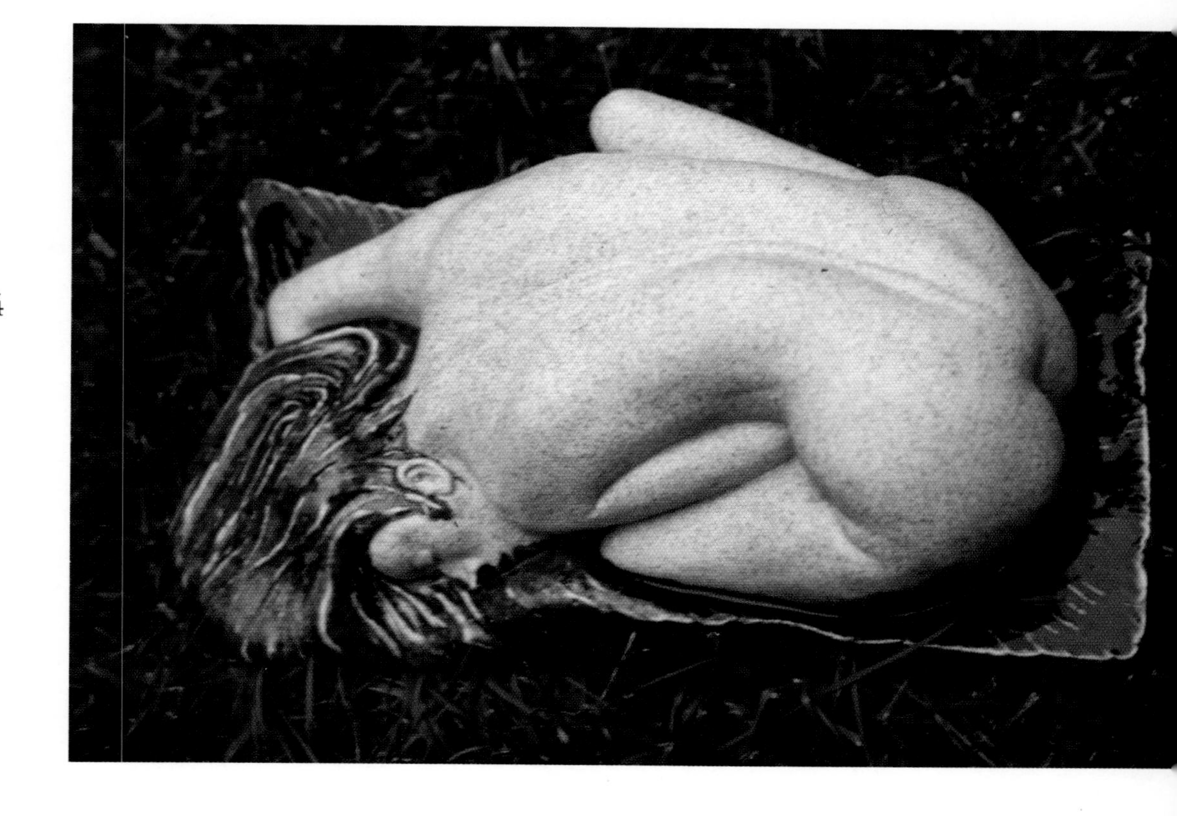

Nostalgic Subject Matter

#145 Zebras

#146

#147

#148

106-8

#149

#150

Three paintings done on the slopes of Mt. Elgon, a dormant volcano on the border of Uganda and Kenya

#151

#152

Tropical Africa has remained vividly clear to me with all those local flavours tourists never perceive.

The reason is that I searched day after day, high and low, for landscape compositions. The main motivation for most of my camping trips was the anticipation of coming upon inspiring landscapes.

Tourists travel by air-conditioned buses from comfortable hotels to game park lodges without really coming into contact with the land and its people. But there are advantages to this separation. The locals are not contaminated by our value system, and the tourists are not exposed to primitive meals, hygiene, toilets.

#153 Precious Clean Water

#154 Two boys getting water from the Nile.

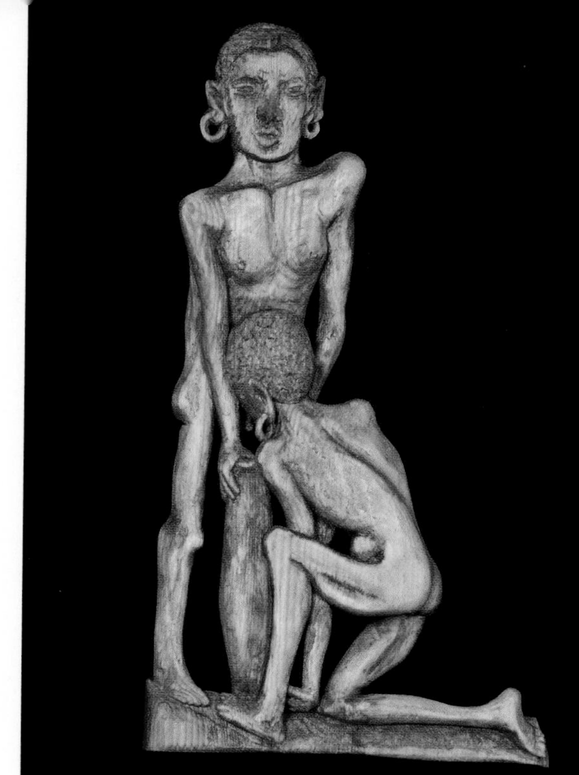

#155 Karamojong women welcoming cattle raiders back home

#156Portrait

The first two years in Africa I painted landscapes and a few still lifes. Those are safe subjects, open to objective observation.

Doing real African life is a different matter.

However, since I was assigned to teach my senior classes imaginative composition which is involved with human activities, I got a quicker initiation into African life. It has fascinated me ever since.

#157

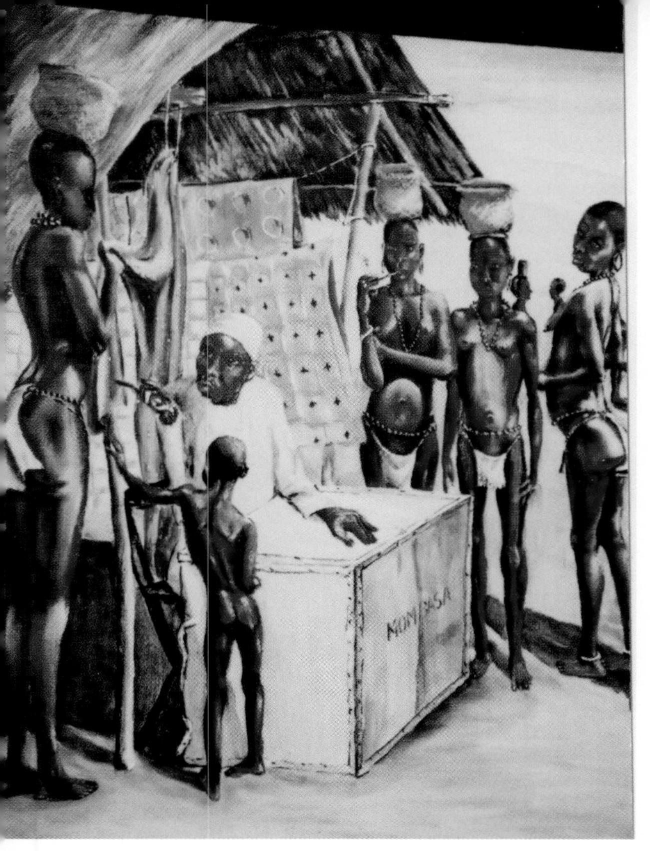

 # 158 Cloth by the yard

#159 Winnowing Sorghum

#160 Rain Shelter

#161

It was always an attractive sight to see a group of women sucking warm beer through long reeds (nowadays plastic tubes). After a while they would add hot water to the brew of millet or sorghum.

The backside of the sculpture with the bored kids is even more exciting to me.

This particular glazed ceramic was purchased by the Ugandan High Commissioner at one of my public exhibitions.

#162

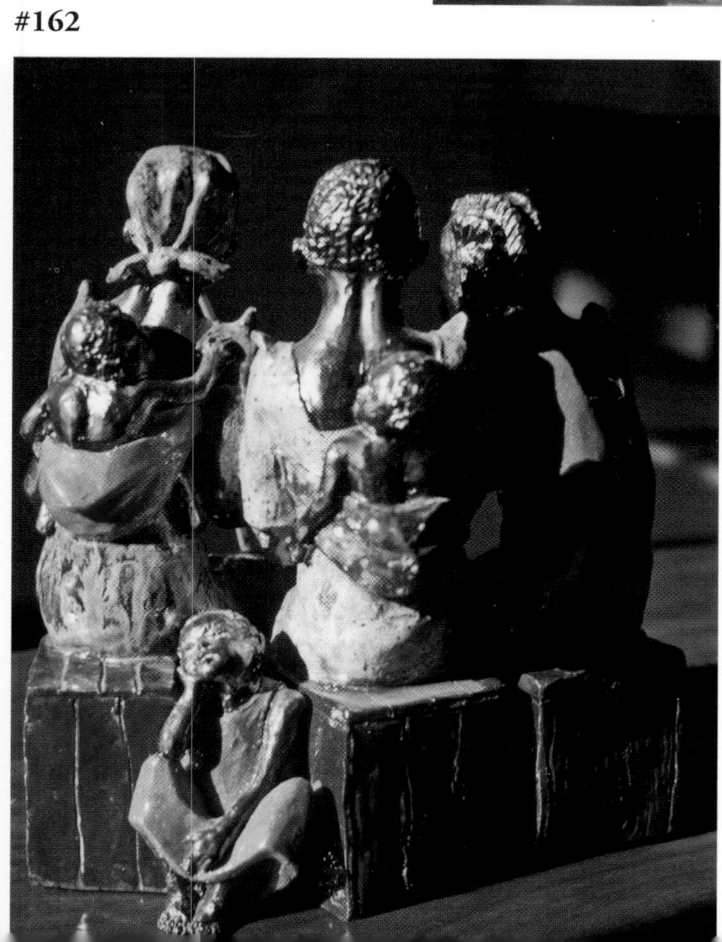

Painting around the world

Wherever I travelled for weeks, I tried to combine my travelling around with painting the local scene.

Italy, Indonesia, and Holland.

Let one painting for each suffice, although for Italy there are three touristy works on pages 86 & 87.

#163

#164

#165

One of the few antique farms on the outskirts of my hometown in Holland.

#166

#167 Sonora Desert

A priest-friend in Phoenix Arizona asked me to take his place for the month of August 1977. Almost every day it was 110° F, but you survive in airconditioning everywhere.

Then I discovered the beauty of the Sonora desert with its starkness and shimmering heat. So each week on my one free day, I would get up at 5 a.m. and be in the desert by six before the real heat of the day. With litres of liquid, I would be finished by noon, and sleep it off in the afternoon.

#168 Arizona Postage Stamp

#169 (top of page) **#170 (lower on page)**

Canadian Landscapes "untouched by human hands"

Why are Canadian artists who live on or near the Canadian shield so predestined to limit themselves to rocks, water, trees and sky for their subject matter? The Group of Seven is a good example. The short answer might lie in the unspoiled emptiness within their horizon, which is becoming rare in today's "Progress of Development".

#171 Last Snow

#172 Pitcher Plants

#173

#174

#175

#176 Village Percée, easternmost Quebec

#177
Farrelton on the Gatineau River

#178 Lanark Swamp

#179

#180

I still have to come across an attractive Russian postage stamp. However, this small, drab, stamp caught my attention: eight sad men pulling a cargo boat down the Volga river. Certainly not an advertisement for the good life under the Soviet regime of 1969.

Then it came to me that this was a painting done by an artist whose name and dates are given in the lower left corner. He lived in the time of the Czars. So this stamp is actually saying: look how bad life was under those oppressive Czars.

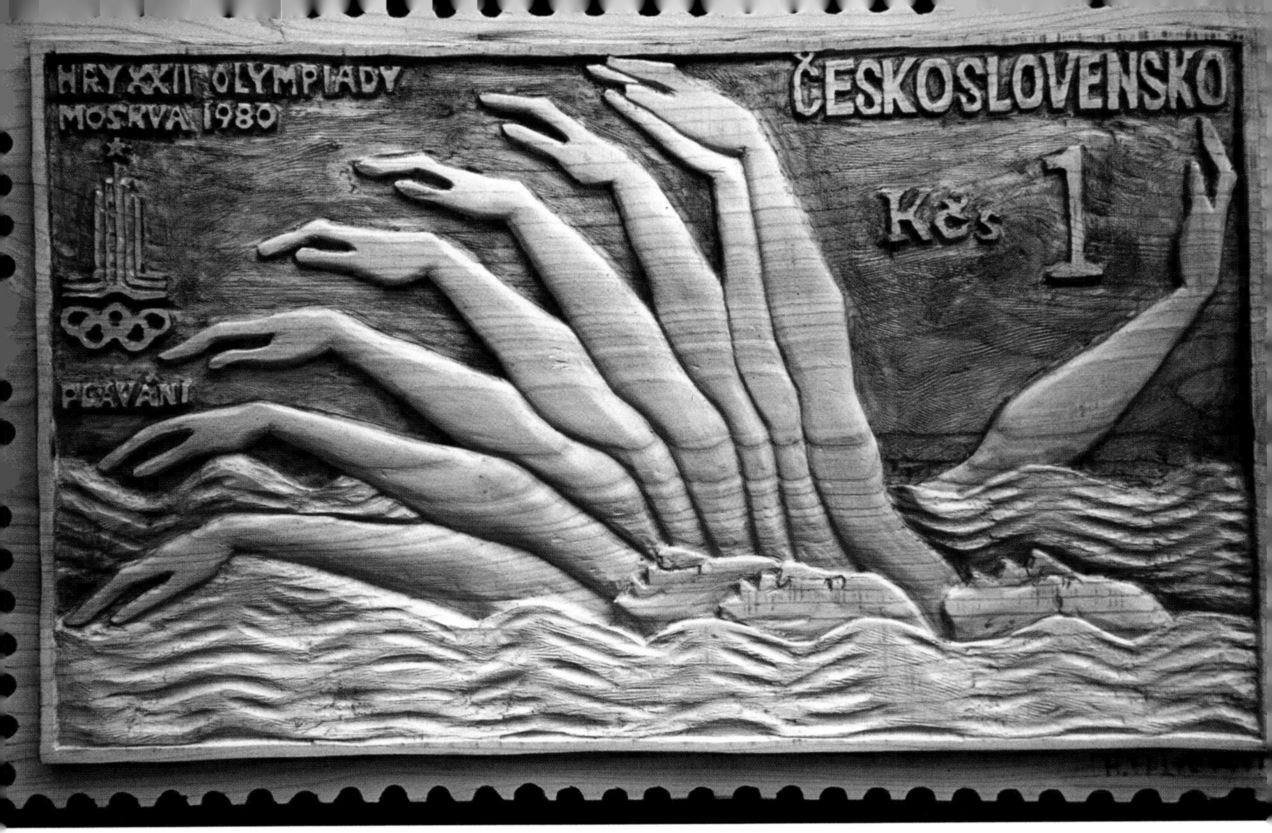

#181

The Olympics always produce a series of fine action poses. The Czechoslovakian stamp of 1980 is highly imaginative.

 # 182

Boys playing with toy boats on a beach.

#183

The U.S. Postal system has produced many attractive stamps, particulary the statehood centennial series, including these three and the three on the following pages.

POSTAGE
3¢
U.S.A.
300 TH ANNIVERSARY OF NEW YORK CITY

#184

ARIZONA
NEW MEXICO
1853
GADSDEN
PURCHASE
MEXICO
RIO GRANDE
TEXAS
3¢ U.S. POSTAGE

#185

#186 Dog sleighs on the surface; submarines below the ice.

#187 Canada failed to issue a Centennial stamp for this Yukon Gold Rush

#188 Pensive

Daydreaming is an effortless form of thinking. But Maria Chapdelaine who is featured on this Canadian postage stamp is too much a pioneer woman to indulge in mindless floating. Not only is she watching the bread she is baking in the outdoors oven, but the broom, basket and box more than just symbolize her domestic chores up north around Lac St. Jean. And even if those chores are done, her hands will never be idle: the needles and wool will grow into a sweater for the long winter ahead. For a moment she even drops her knitting on her lap as some long-term concern seems to call for all her attention.

The poetical setting belies the seriousness of living in less complicated days before cars, electricity and radio.

POSTES CANADA POSTAGE
WHOOPING CRANE
GRUE BLANCHE
5¢

#189

4¢
CANADA
CARIBOU
3¢
POSTES POSTAGE
CANADA

#190

#191

#192 Montreal

#193 Ottawa

#194 Château Laurier

#195

#196 Outport on the Labrador Coast

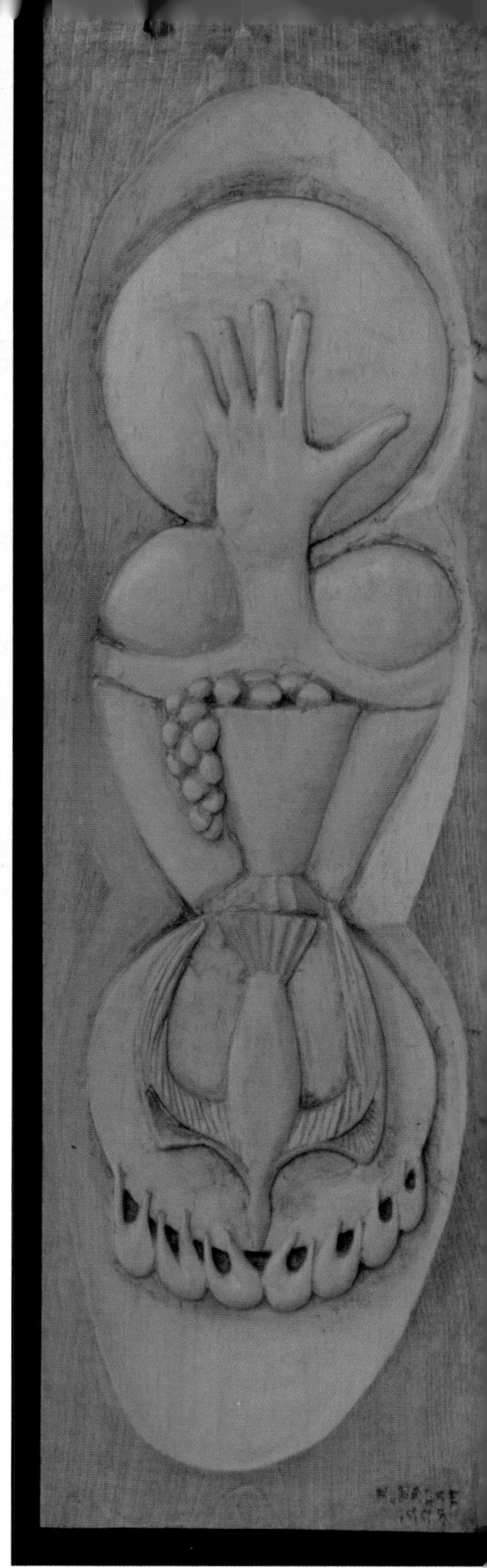

#197

Institutions requesting a symbol, or logos:

top left: The Canadian Conference of Catholic Bishops

 # 198

Proposed logo for Catholic Trinity High School

#199

Ecumenical chapels in hospitals requesting logos in free arrangement, or in form of a wheelchair wheel with spokes leading the the One God as Ottawa Civic did.

#200

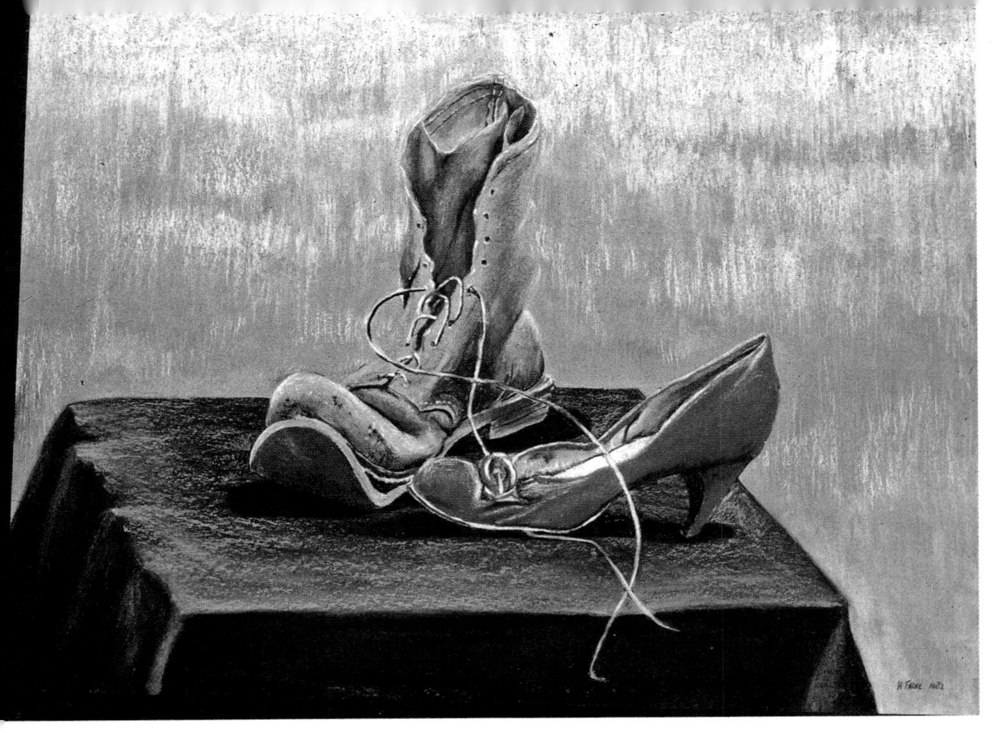

#201 Wedding present for farming couple.

#202

#203

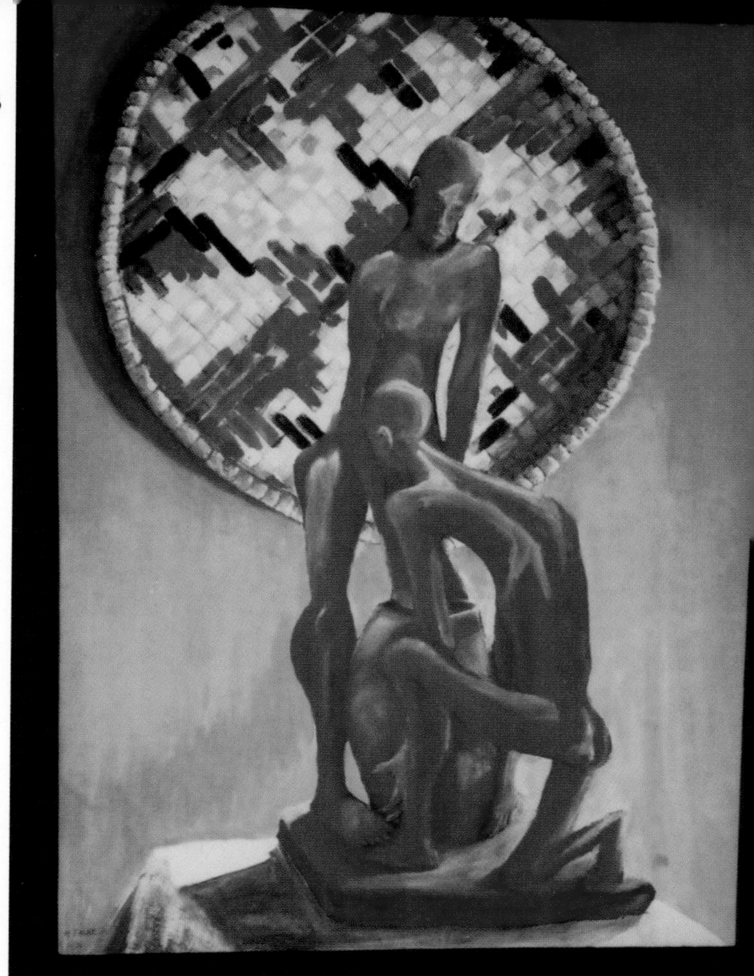

Still life painting is the best way for getting into painting. It trains you for composing, for precise observation and finally translating it into colour.

And always the objects are in front of you, challenging and criticizing you.

#204 Still Life with Basket

#205 From a National Arts Centre poster

#206

#207 Two boys running

#208 Three boys running

#209 Yugoslav Quartet

#210 Three Girls Dancing

#211

Two Ceramic Sketches of Log Drives

#212

#213 Antelopes

#214 Horses

#215 Horses

Ten Solitudes

#216

Loneliness

In spite of cell phones and instant messaging, we modern people suffer the pain of loneliness and yearning for meaningful connection. Creative artists are exposing this frequently in novels, songs and paintings How do we deal with this pain?

The bulk of our modern rock music provides a temporal shield to drown out the pain of our loneliness by booming rhythms and clanging guitars. Besides, the writhing lead singers scream into their mikes, and drown out every private thinking and emotion. It is as if the audience are on drugs and let go of themselves briefly.

The danger is that if we do not deal with loneliness, it may lead us to become hardened and desensitized persons, continuously searching for more and higher kicks. Lonely people cruising the nightspots and ending up with bad company with those whom they hope to alleviate their loneliness.

"Ten Solitudes" bunches together in the compact space around a kitchen table a number of dissatisfactions in ordinary life: hiding behind a newspaper, absorbed in a toy or tv program or hairdo, an undefined feeling of emptiness, an outreach for anyone outside by phone.

#217 Ceramic sketch of people waiting for transportation

#218 Soup Kitchen: Line-up of solitary individuals, including the tortured Christ

Artistically speaking, I love old towns and old castles. In my last book of 2008, "Sculpture Swan Songs", I devoted a section to these old towns. However, I added a biblical caution: "The typical Hebrew is a nomadic herdsman. He distrusts city life as an attempt to escape from the vigilance of God, and as looking for anonymity and self-protection behind stone walls. So many misfits in rural society escaped to the city (as is the case even today) to make city life even more suspect. Their arch-enemies, the Philistines, lived in cities. Sodom and Gomorrah were symbols of everything that could go wrong with city life. Nineveh, Babylon and later Rome, were all despised by them. Even Jerusalem, their only city, was merely tolerated as a necessity for temple rituals. "Come out of Babylon, my people", is a shout heard repeatedly from Genesis to Revelations, "you must not take part in their sins, you must not share in her punishment." *Rev. 18:2*

#219 "Lost in the Crowd"

In the painting "Lost in the crowd", I used the central characters of Tooker's masterpiece, and then I used the given space of the wings to illustrate various forms of modern isolation. People are imprisoned in their own fabrications. They live in perpetual noise that prevents any private reflection, any meditation, any authentic intercommunication. All are moving around, looking for something that is missing, but not knowing what.

Jesus looks at the crowd and pities them, for they are like sheep without a shepherd. Usually Jesus meets the multitude when they have left their towns and follow him into the desert. *Matt. 14:13*

#220 Pontius Pilate

Pontius Pilate, before washing his hands, agonizing over his decision to toss off Jesus as just another common criminal.

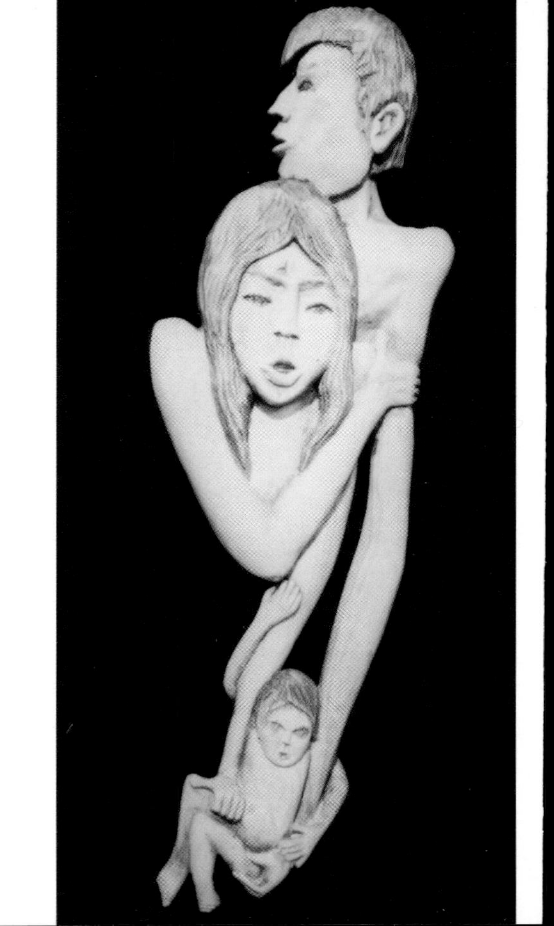

#221 "What to do?"

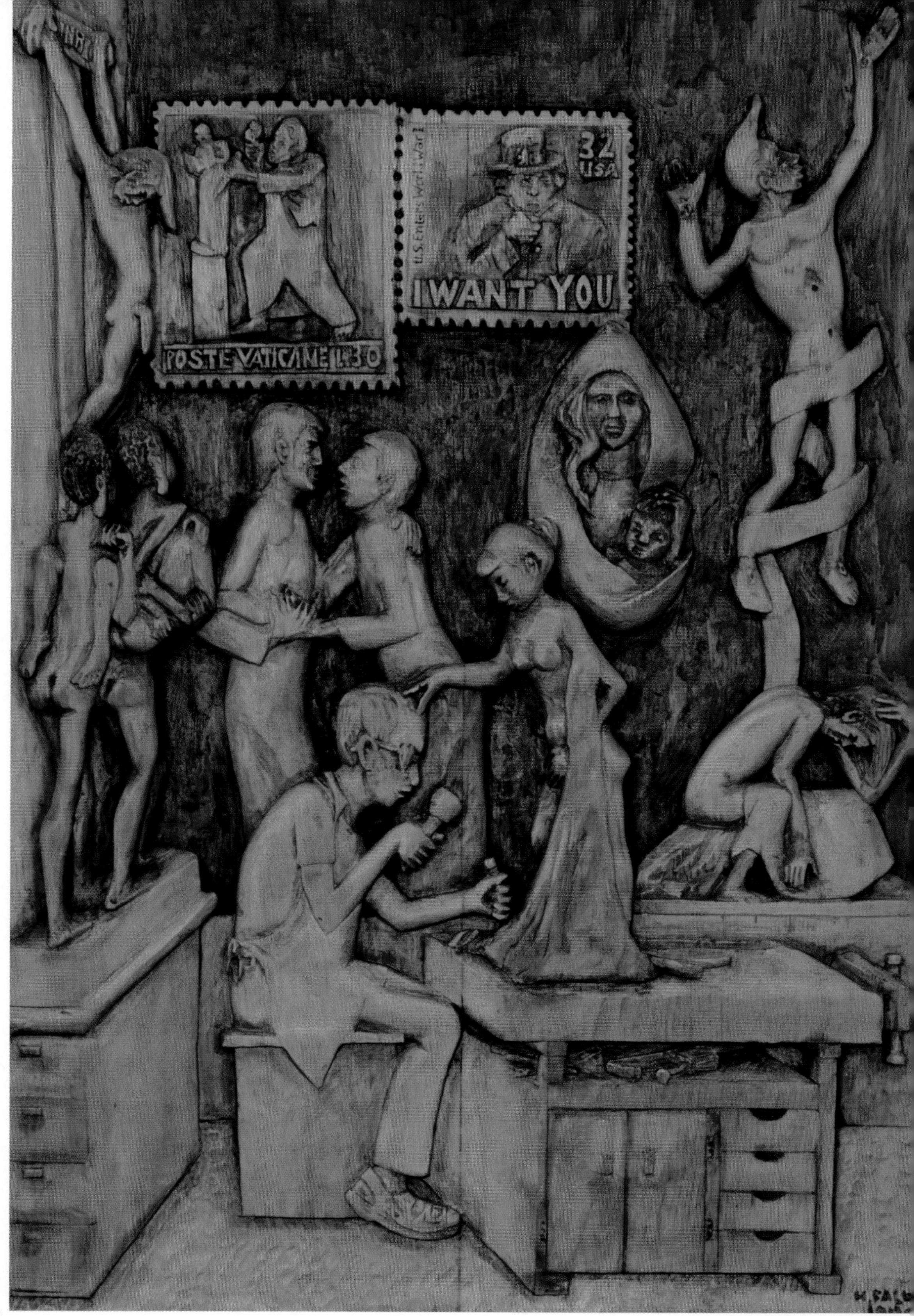

#222

Probably my favourite sculpture... "In My Studio"

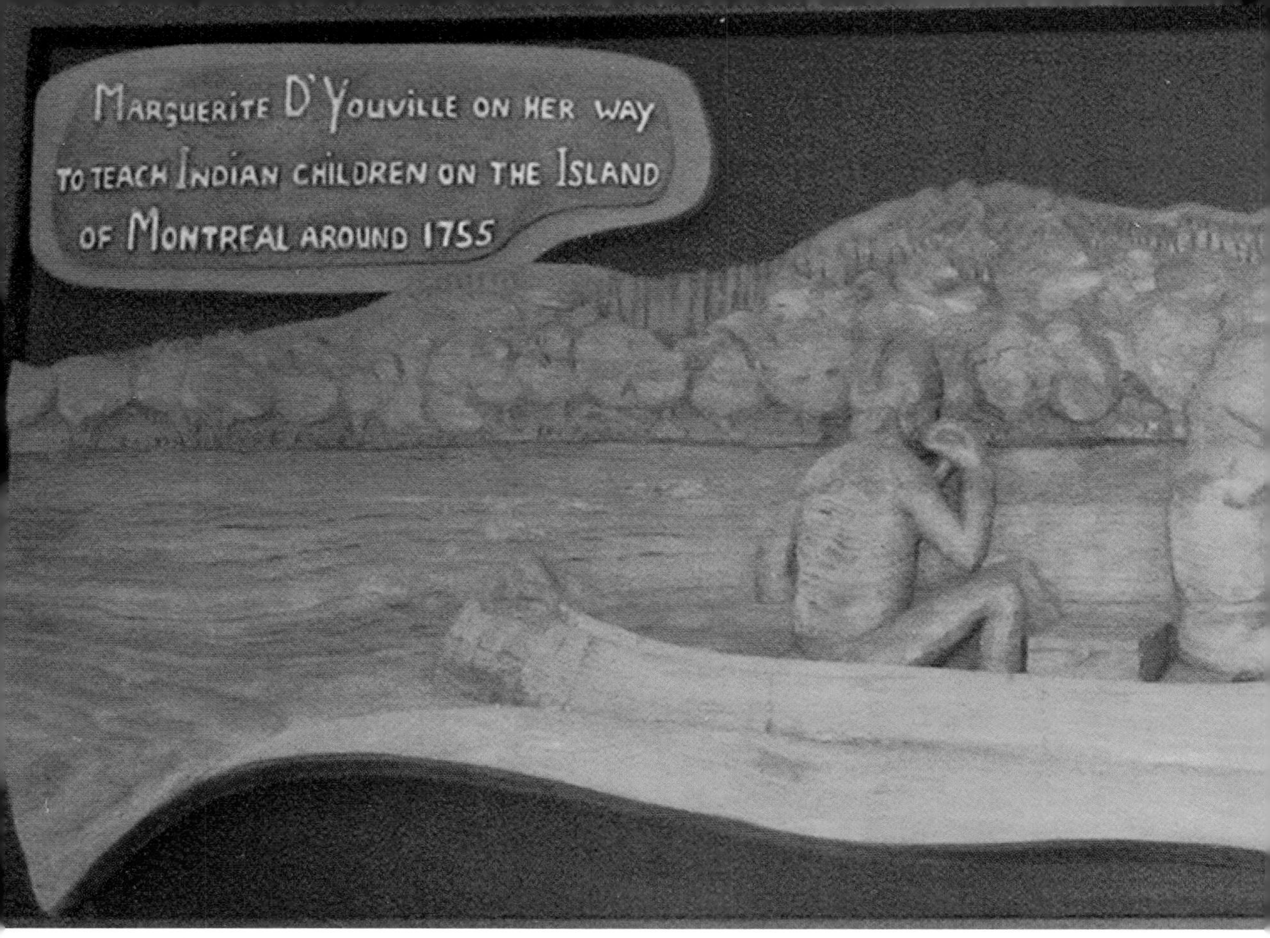

Last minute Gleanings

#223 (above)

#224

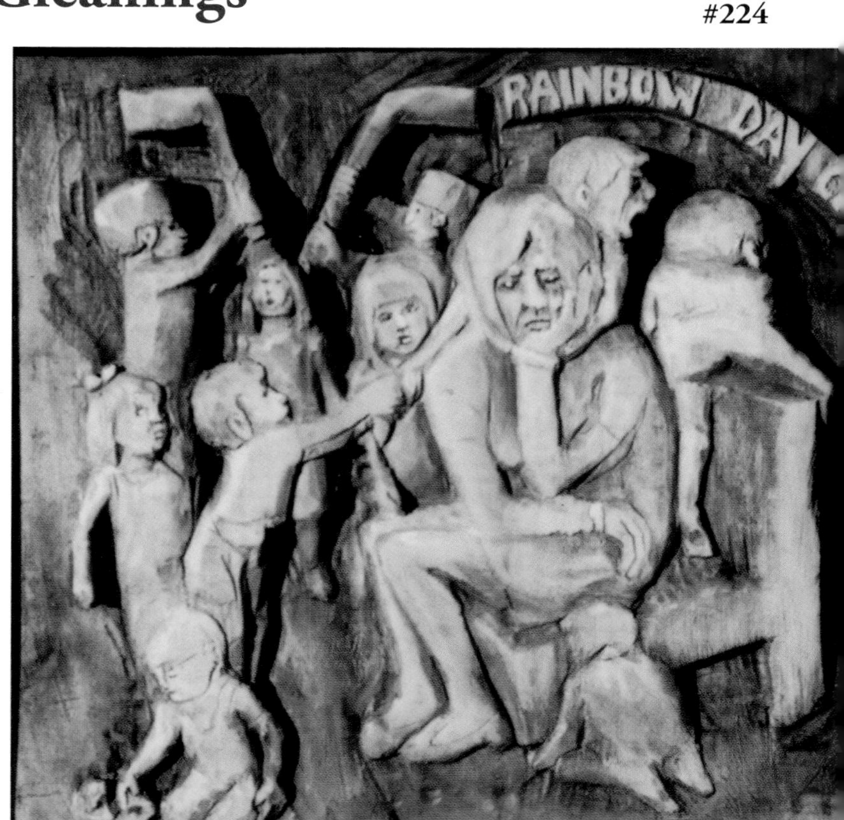

In my attempts to glean up some of the sculptures that have escaped the photographer, because they were given away spontaneously, I was fortunate to pick up a few good ones within the parishes, for instance "The Professional Babysitter" owned by Joan Hawco, but especially Theresa Kelly's three Shakespearean heroines which were completed in stages.

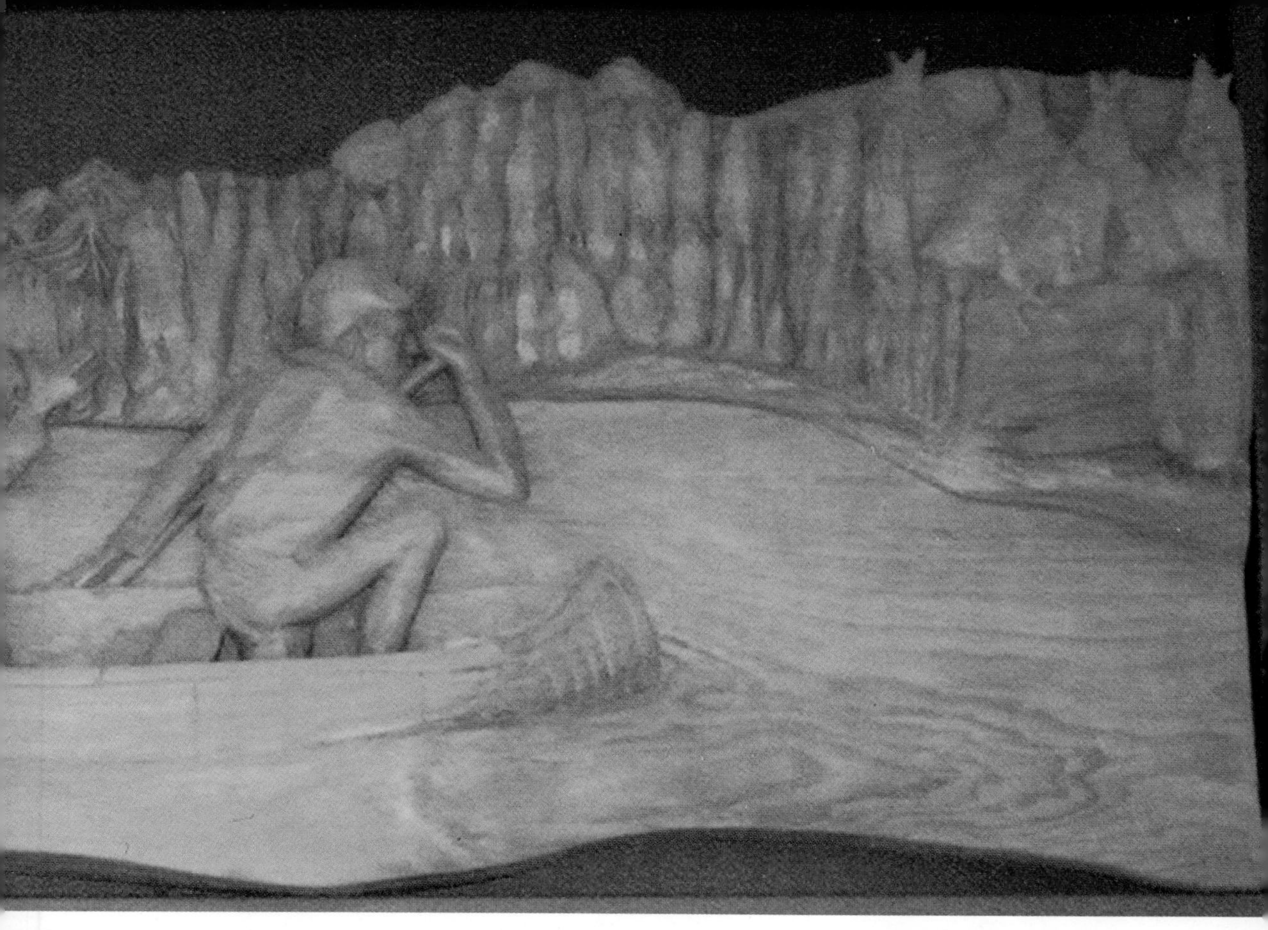

#225

Jesus raising the only son of the widow of Naim.

Others will remain un-gleaned because they are a bit cumbersome (Serafinis), or mounted in Catholic schools. "St. Marguerite d'Youville" was gleaned in the nick of time by Daphne Sandre who teaches at that school.

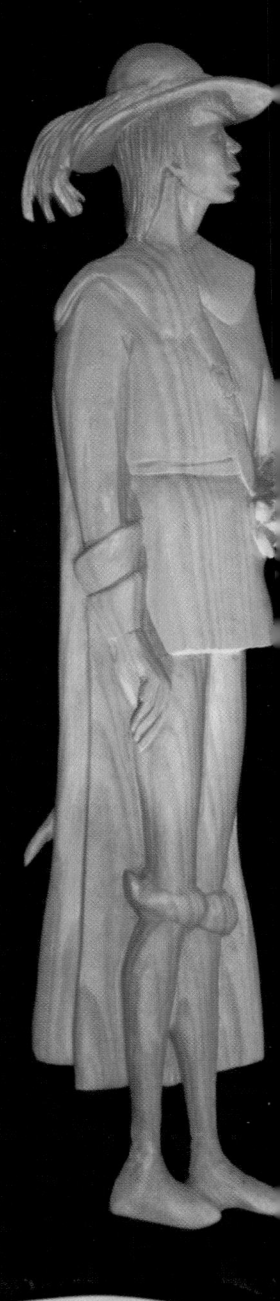

#226

"O LOOK UPON ME, SIR,
AND HOLD YOUR HANDS
IN BENEDICTION O'ER ME.
NO, SIR, YOU MUST NOT KNEEL."

"LADY, YOU ARE THE CRUEL'ST
SHE ALIVE, IF YOU WILL
LEAD THESE GRACES
TO THE GRAVE,
AND LEAVE THE WORLD
NO COPY."

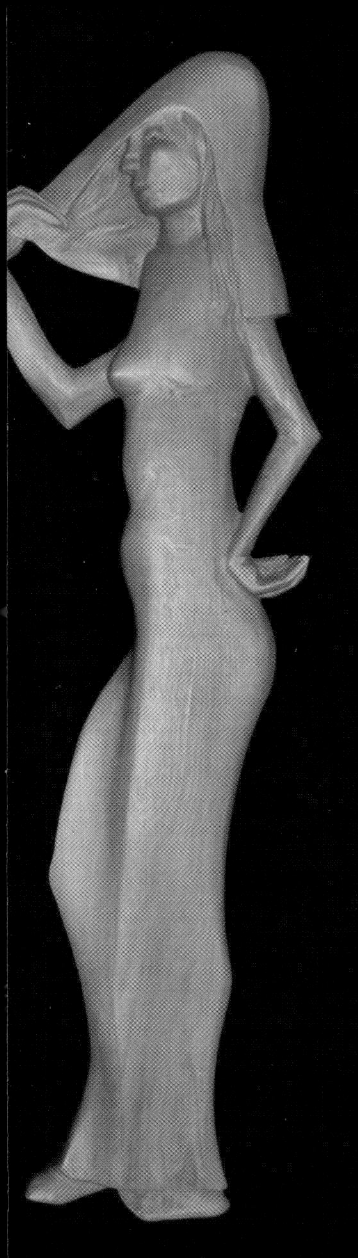

#227

#228

#229 December, 2009, my last painting before the deadline of this book: Sketch of a detail of Winslow Homer's "Eight Bells"

Annotations on selected art work

#1(cover) Gleaning was the prerogative of poor people. In the Old Testament Book of Ruth, 2:14, Boaz was quickly smitten with this needy but attractive foreigner, and even ordered his workers to "pull out some heads of grain from the bundles and leave them for her to pick up."

#4 Adam and Eve, still in God's hands. Stoneware done in 1980 in preparation for a bronze version. Because of its complicated undercuts, I could extract only a single copy.

#5 Adam and Eve, when it dawns upon them that they are in trouble. The stoneware is most suitable, as it comes close to real skin.

#17 Mary is portrayed as somewhat timid, and almost shying away from the angel. If I remember correctly, I borrowed this posture from Rosetti of the Pre-Raphaelite painters. It has had its influence on my Annunciation in #19.

#21 This white pine sculpture pictures the arrival of visitors from the East. St. Matthew states, "when they saw the same star again over the stable, they rejoiced with exceeding joy." Mt. 2:9

#36&37 Two opposite views of the same sculpture illustrate the parable of the rich man and Lazarus. It is one meter high and constructed with firm wires that are anchored into the wooden base. The surface is papier maché over chicken wire. It won a first prize at a Toronto exhibition in 1990, and was eagerly requested as a donation by a society that works for rehabilitation of alcooholics and drug addicts in large industries.

#62&63 The victims were urged to drug themselves, partly also to diminish the pain of having their legs broken with a club and then being dragged in the swamp by crocodiles. There is a parallel on Calvary where the three to be crucified are offered the same kind of mercy drink. Jesus sips and then declines. In other words, he shows appreciation for the gesture of compassion, but then refuses to be drugged into numbness and wooziness.

#71 Scripture references to Jesus' crucifixion are unanimous in declaring that he hung on the cross naked. For up to six hours his genitals and bodily excretions were out in the open: one more reason to avoid cloth. The references either briefly state that he was hung naken to a tree, or that he was stripped and his clothes divided among the guards. St. Paul writes that Jesus "did not cling to his equality with God but emptied himself to assume the condition of a slave." (Phil. 2:6-7) That was literally fulfilled.

#73. This painting won an award as the best magazine cover. The actual ecumenical magazine, *Grail*, folded some 10 years ago.

#80 As a good-bye present to Immaculata High School, I painted a mural for the students' dining hall. It illustrates St. Francis' *Canticle of the Sun*, in which he praises God for the beauties of the created world, from the fish in the water up to the birds and clouds in the sky.

#81 Canterbury Tales of Chaucer:
I used a slab of golden ash, over 4 ft. long, and carved the silhouette of all the pilgrims and letters, before painting the scene.

#202 Around 1985, I took courses in watercolour painting. The teacher was most meticulous about design, and where the colours were to be placed on the palette. He had visited abandoned mining camps in the Yukon and put before us these rusty coffee cans.

#206 A dynamic ballet pose is irresistible for me as a sculptor. This one of ballerina Suzanne Farrell was taken from Time magazine. I quote, "the willowy star was that rarest of rarities, a classical dancer with a chorus girl's legs. She was also Director George Balanchine's special protégée..."

#210 Here is another sculpture constructed with wire and *papier mâché*, like the Lazarus of #36 & 37. To my surprise, it was selected for the front cover of the "Living with Christ" missal, under the title "Alleluia".

#221 What to do? Here is a sculpture conceived as an open question with no definite answer. Will we be able to raise this child properly? Are we as a couple perhaps too interested in just each other?

Herman Falke, S.C.J., S.S.C.

- S.C. J. in 1948, joined the Sacred Heart Fathers, at age 20.
- S.S. C. Life member of the Sculptors Society of Canada, and eight years in the Executive as treasurer.
- Taught Art and English in high schools for 35 years.
- Author of five art books, and co-author of four more in Dutch.
- Painter and sculptor of the “human landscape.”
- Entomologist in the insect world.
- Travelled widely in Africa, Asia, and Western Europe, speaking four languages.
- Loved camping, canoeing, and collecting berries and wild mushrooms.
- Since 1992 pastor of St. Brigid’s and St. John’s in the Ottawa-Osgoode area.
- Blessed with good health, he has had a life full of creativity, communication and reflection.

These last gleanings reflect much of that.

1996

2004

2008

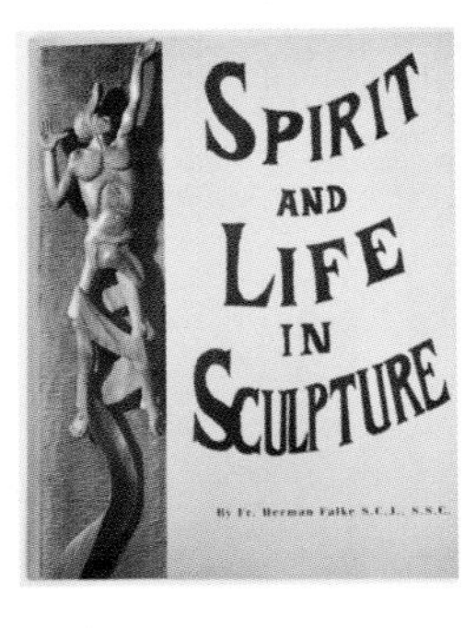

1999

2007

2009